FENG SHUI
in the
Garden

FENG SHUI
in the
Garden

Simple Solutions

for Creating Comforting,

Life-Affirming Gardens

of the Soul

Nancilee Wydra

Plant Suggestions and Illustrations by
Bridget Skinner, Landscape Designer

CONTEMPORARY BOOKS

Library of Congress Cataloging-in-Publication Data

Wydra, Nancilee.
    Feng shui in the garden : simple solutions for creating comforting, life-affirming gardens of the soul / Nancilee Wydra.
       p.   cm.
    Includes bibliographical references and index.
    ISBN 0-8092-3055-0
     1. Gardening.   2. Gardening—Philosophy.   3. Feng-shui.
I. Title.
SB455.W93   1997
712'.2—dc21   96-52369
                                                                  CIP

Cover design by Monica Baziuk
Cover photograph copyright © Roger Foley. Garden designed by Ellen Penick.
Interior design by Mary Lockwood
Interior illustration by Bridget Skinner
Chapter opening art by Lydia Neinart
Photo of Nancilee Wydra by Suzan Phillips
Photo of Bridget Skinner by John L. Blom

15   14   13   12   11   10   9   8   7   6   5

To my dear friends Mark, Lynn, Chloe, and Barnaby Sharrock-Root, who taught me the meaning of nurturing. I am deeply grateful for the joy they have brought into my life.

To Sandy Vidan for the enduring gift of a lifetime of friendship.

To Regula Noetzli for inspiring this book.

To Uma Gray's gifts. May she bestow the same upon herself.

To Paul Lorber, who taught me about the earth, I am indebted.

And to Mom and Dad, Robyn and Zachary, for letting me tell their stories.

A special thanks to Adrienne S. Neal, 6262 Savannah Drive, Melbourne Village, Florida 32904, historic landscape designer and feng shui professional, whose ideas and plant suggestions added to this book.

To Bridget Skinner, for her drawings and knowledge of which plants to place in the gardens, my gratitude.

And to Bill. May his wish come true.

An imaginary scene somewhere in Wonderland . . .

"What did you say?" cried Alice, "That a flower is a mirror of me?"

"Yes," said the Hatter, as he stood on his head. "We're an upside-down, inside-out plant!"

"What! Don't confuse me!" Alice implored as she bent her head between her legs to view the Hatter eye-to-eye.

"Well, they breathe in what we exhale and furthermore, exhale what we need. Their roots face the earth's center, while our brain sits on the tippy top of our bodies. Our reproductive organs are hidden in the bottom of our body and their reproductive organs are exposed for all to see on top. So, if you want to be a plant then you are completely wrong."

"Well," said Alice, "so much for my being a flower. I shan't even think about it anymore."

And with a huff she stood up and turned to walk away.

The Hatter looked at the silhouette of Alice as it receded down the pebble-lined path and noticed a red floppy flower bouncing and bobbing on the brim of her hat.

CONTENTS

INTRODUCTION

Feng shui, an ancient Chinese discipline, examines the relationships between person and place. By emphasizing how a place will be experienced emotionally and physically, feng shui shifts the experience of place away from a reaction to pure design and control to a cooperation between person and place. Alliance with all things brings harmony, while domination brings discord and disaster. To benefit from nature's intention, we need to discard the notion of control and replace it with partnership.

Nowhere is this partnership more evident than in a garden. A garden is a detailed room complete with walls and a ceiling. A garden can be a shared space, like a gathering room, or a private space, like a bedroom. Its elements include line, color, touch, sight, and smell. All these properties have inherent in them messages that can propel us toward contentment if we heed the principles governing their use. Consider the feeling of a frigid New England winter day when glancing out the window at a red-twig dogwood. The contrast of a red bark silhouetted against chalky expanses of lawn can evoke cheer and energy because the vibration of red exceeds all other colors in intensity and action. By attending to the principles of feng shui, we can create areas that respond to our needs and elicit emotions deep within our soul. By disregarding the impact of the principles of feng shui, we sidestep a natural ally.

The two Chinese characters for feng shui literally signify "wind" and "water," but as with many Chinese terms, the meaning eludes an easy interpretation. What surrounds us seeps into our pores and saturates our lives. A lush garden can nurture, as can a fragile, arid landscape, as long as each is in tune with its surroundings. On the other hand, devastation and decay can damage the spirit as surely as a wrecking ball can fell a mighty building. By implementing the concepts contained within feng shui, we can increase our opportunity for thriving. By substituting control with partnership, we connect with the *spirit of place* and, in doing so, are in harmony with the grander scheme.

Perhaps you have a memory of a place that fastens itself to your spirit and links you to the wonders of the smells, textures, and sights of this earth. As a child of the city, natural phenomena were truly a mystery to me. I was seven years old before I saw a tuna that didn't come from a can. My father and I had tiptoed out of our rented summer cottage away from our slumbering family to visit a misty New England pier. The tuna was lying in the belly of a fishing boat that had returned from an early morning run in cold, choppy waters. I was amazed that the actual fish was a hundred times larger than the cans resting on the shelves of my mother's pantry.

When I was seven years old, we moved to New Jersey to live atop a mountain that rose like a turtle's shell from the flat fertile valley of the Hudson River. The back door of my sturdy Tudor home opened onto a yard that sloped dramatically to the street. Many summer days I would surrender to impulse by plopping down on the freshly cut grass and rolling down the hill. Flying by beds of flowers that were surrounded by rocks holding their island turf in place, the freshness of smells, the smoothness of grass punctuated by the sting of pebbles hiding like gnomes, and the giddiness of the descent would delight me for hours.

Stately, fragrant trees lined the serpentine street. Wide sidewalks were buffered with thick belts of grass. Dandelions sprinkled lawns and crept into cracks that split the sidewalks. It was in this home, standing at the edge of the woods, that I learned to love, respect, and be in awe of nature.

During childhood hours spent gazing at pictures of flowers and exploring the fields, woods, and gardens in my neighborhood, my dreams and desires began to crystallize. Away from the influences of people and unencumbered by anything but my own imagination, my inner being blossomed. The outdoors became a place for me to dream.

> *Help me dream, my sweet rose bush;*
> *Unveil life's velvety, vibrant blush;*
> *Teach me to love while I care,*
> *And be cautious even as I dare.*
>
> *Anonymous*

Woven through our personal memory is a grander intelligence, one that cultivates a system embracing joy, as well as sustainability. Inherent in this is respect for the genius of place. For example, planting water-loving grasses in Arizona strikes a discordant note in the natural surroundings and taxes limited water resources of the region. Being in tune with the genius of place requires recognizing and valuing a harmonious environment. It means knowing the characteristics of the vegetation of the area.

Using vegetation's talents can also benefit our health. Peppermint plants not only can spice iced tea with a snappy zing, but also, when planted by an entrance door, can prevent flies from entering our house. No need for pesticides that exude toxins into our air to destroy our health. Whether it's the micro or macro human experience, it is in our best interest to merge with what is, in order to reap benefits.

Only when we discard the notion of superiority over the natural world will we be able to live in contentment and harmony. By understanding the essence expressed in each life-form, we will benefit from its genius.

The longest-running show off Broadway, *The Fantastiks,* has a song with the words "Plant a cabbage, get a cabbage, not a brussel sprout. That's why I love vegetables, you know what they're about. . . . The man who plants a garden is a very happy man." Surely happiness is at the confluence of contentment and contribution. Few other places give us the chance to merge the opportunity of intention and reward as a garden does. While it's difficult to capture the entire meaning of how a garden can make us feel, it is not far removed from the poet Pope's "Genius of Place":

> *Consult the Genius of the Place in all;*
> *That tells the Waters or to rise, or fall;*
> *Or helps th' ambitious Hill the heav'ns to scale,*
> *Or scoops in circling theatres the Vale;*
> · · · · · · · · · · · ·
> *Paints as you plant, and, as you work, designs.*
> *Alexander Pope*

There is no substitute for feeling the crunchy soil roll through your fingers as you part the earth's flesh to accept a seed. From the delicate stalk of the seedling to the blossom of maturity, plants furnish us with so much more than they demand. The wisdom contained within feng shui can be applied to aid us in securing the best for ourselves as we cross the threshold from our indoor to outdoor home.

To this end, I have prepared the book in two parts: the first to provide background on the principles of feng shui and how they relate to the elements of a garden and the second to describe special gardens that are designed to resonate and respond to specific needs. If you already know what you want and need in a garden, you may begin with the second part. If you are new to the philosophy embodied in feng shui, you will benefit from the knowledge in the first part.

In the first part, you will discover elements that combine to create a garden that will add significantly to your life's experiences: ingredients that add movement and energy; qualities that contribute clarity and intrigue; shapes, colors, and symbolic meanings that truly help you create a garden of the soul. You will also discover that how and where you place the elements in your garden will reflect back to the areas of your life. Finally, you will learn about plants that run amok if you are not careful, as well as about plants that can clean your environment by consuming toxins.

The second part provides descriptions of eight special gardens: the power garden, meditation garden, lover's garden, healing garden, child's garden, fertility garden, winter's garden, and retirement garden. Each garden is a tangible example of the application of the principles discussed in the first part of the book.

Once you are inspired to begin creating your special gardens, Appendix A, a master list of plants, will help you select trees, shrubs, and annuals and perennials, as well as vines and ground cover, that correspond to specific principles of feng shui regarding shape and movement. (You can also see at a glance which plants will protect your garden from ravenous deer!) Appendix B, color plant charts, will assist in identifying plants that add color to your garden in each of the four seasons.

It is my intention for this book to be the vehicle to help you achieve all that you wish for yourself and your loved ones . . . and more.

Give yourself a gift of a garden for your soul!

FENG SHUI
in the
Garden

Part 1

INGREDIENTS FOR THE GARDEN

1

GARDENS OF THE SOUL

A garden connects us with the wheel of life in a direct, measurable way. Because our endeavors are only in part influenced by our input, we learn through experience that effort doesn't always equal reward. Sometimes, weather patterns, creatures, or what seems like the whims of fate deal us a bad hand. We have gained in wisdom when we understand that the process is as satisfying as the sought-after result.

When my son told me he was training to run a marathon and described jogging through automobile-filled streets, I pictured cars whisking past him as he consumed large amounts of exhaust fumes because his breath was deepened by exertion.

"Zachary," I suggested, "why not select a jogging route through a field or a park or around a local football stadium that would be less dangerous?" Certainly, I thought, the road to victory should be paved with pleasant, healthy experiences that enhance the nanosecond of glory while crossing the finish line. Why persist in chasing a brief moment of satisfaction if the process is not enjoyable?

Yet, persistence can be exactly the characteristic that enables us to achieve positive results. The proverbial "overnight" successes are usually people who are not daunted by setbacks or defeats. The more we march unswervingly toward a goal, the more likely we are to reach it.

Gardening, too, is a labor of possibilities. The more time we invest, the more we glean.

If we are to benefit from our labor, we must learn to positively interpret messages along the way. Nerves are connected by impulses, or messages, that travel through apparently empty spaces. Messages travel from one nerve ending to the other by jumping across the spaces in between with an energy likened to electrical impulses. These messages constantly leap from one nerve ending to another throughout our lives. In the same way, our surroundings infuse us with either positive or negative messages. Just as a monotone voice can be drowned out by a choir of singers, negative impulses can be squelched by positive ones.

While "now" is the only moment we have, we are trailed by the sum of our past and are connected to the future by the forces of effort and inspiration. In both cases, the leap is propelled by energy transmitted through what surrounds us. We can benefit by being encircled by positive messages.

The Chinese would describe this process as the Tao (the way things are and the way they work). We are no more separated from the sum of our past than we are from the potential of our future. Although we cannot see what lies ahead, the way we seek to propel ourselves into our future influences the outcome. Creating gardens to express our heart's desires connects us to the energy and opportunity of all things. The unlimited potential of the Tao is expressed in every moment we share with a garden.

Along with the Tao, or connectedness, feng shui examines chi, or energy, and yin/yang, or balance. Through these underpinnings the building blocks of feng shui are fashioned. The pyramid school of feng shui reveals the essentials of this ancient discipline without the mitigating factors of culture, generation, and geography. Know that who you are and your own unique life experiences must be added to the mix just as soil, rainfall, and climate must be taken into account for vegetation selection.

A garden can be both a catalyst and a mirror of our personal energy as well as a reflection of the place. Creating a garden helps balance our lives. To be outdoors involved in an activity that requires physical and mental exertion is sorely needed in a culture that orchestrates most activities indoors. Time spent outdoors gives us time for contemplation, time to refurbish our path with those ingredients likely to propel us toward happiness.

A garden of the soul transforms the moment and shapes the future.

2

FENG SHUI'S PHILOSOPHIES FOR THE GARDEN

Every experience in life is stirred by the hand of place. Feng shui suggests that the spaces we inhabit influence our lives in such a profound way that to not pay attention to our surroundings could be as damaging as neglecting to dress a wound. According to the Chinese, our living spaces are enmeshed with our capacity to be happy as surely as they are with our physical disposition and our social and economic conditions. Where we live and work can either hinder or help us toward a successful life's journey.

Traditional books on feng shui do not address the landscape in depth. They normally mention the advisability of a winding rather than straight path to an entrance and give some guidelines about positioning a home to face southeast and be protected by a hill to the north. These books suggest that only those living in rugged mountainous terrain can have ideal feng shui conditions. To traditionalists, a site without a dragon-shaped mountain to the east and a tiger shape to the west would be less than ideal. Other general guidelines about healthy vegetation are usually mentioned. For example, if a tree needs to be cut down or is uprooted by natural conditions, it is advisable to replace it immediately. However, when all is said and done, the ideas contained within traditional feng shui do not reveal how to integrate its principles into landscapes or gardens.

To prevent feng shui from becoming an arcane discipline, its principles must be distilled to their essences. Whether or not we live with mountains or have landscape features that mimic those in China, we can all benefit by enhancing outdoor spaces.

Here are some basic tenets that can be applied to any landscape surrounding a home.

Ten Essentials of Feng Shui for Landscaping a Home

1. Protect the home from severe weather by natural vegetation, topography, or fences.
2. Site it above flooding and spring runoffs.
3. Place the most frequently used exit door facing the direction of the rising sun.
4. Create curved pathways.
5. Create a threshold that separates the public domain from the private one.
6. Ensure that healthy vegetation surrounds the home.
7. Replace all trees and plants that either die or need to be cut down.
8. Maintain a balance of vegetation between too sparse and too overgrown.
9. Block out large ominous objects that face the property.
10. Ensure privacy.

A garden is an outdoor room. While a garden can be a wondrous connection to nature, it can also be an important self-help tool. It can translate what we know, need, and expect in fresh ways. Just as an old dress or suit can be transformed by new accessories, we can be remade when we are given fresh opportunities to view life from a different perspective.

A garden's room will have a point of entry and a way to reach a comfortable place to partake in the room's activity. A garden needs a path leading to it, a threshold or door to enter, walls to define the space, and a place for repose.

We do not think it strange to expect each room in our home to enhance a particular activity. We expect a bedroom to be relaxing, a gathering room to encourage conversation, and a dining room to be fitting for the consumption of food. Why shouldn't outdoor spaces function in the same way?

In addition to providing a forum for nature's wonders, a garden can help us be all we want to be. By designing outdoor spaces to fulfill specific intentions, we enhance the likelihood of achieving sought-after goals. A garden can be a partner in fulfilling desires. We can encourage healing, inspire personal power, and reinforce love in an outdoor setting.

The rewards gained by creating a garden match the efforts expended. Connectedness, balance, and energy are the key concepts of feng shui and can be applied to an outdoor setting. Traditional feng shui calls these areas the Tao (connectedness), yin/yang (balance), and chi (energy).

CONNECTEDNESS, OR THE TAO

Our unique connections to our geographic location, culture, generation, family association, and sex are important ingredients to consider when designing any environment. To help understand the staggering scope of connectedness, I have broken it down into two categories: horizontal and vertical.

Horizontal Connectedness

Horizontal connectedness is that which exists at the moment. It is winter as I finish this book; therefore, my horizontal connection to the seasons is winter. Each winter is similar, but not exactly the same each year. Last year I was on a skiing vacation, while this year I sit in front of my computer. We are connected horizontally to the people in our homes, our careers, the seasons, and what happens in the here and now. Horizontal connections may or may not be enduring, but at any given moment they must be factored in.

Vertical Connectedness

Vertical connections are in the past, like childhood memories. They are threads that continue to run through our lives. I will never smell a lilac without remembering walking to my childhood home's back door underneath a trellis that was weighed down with lilac blooms cascading in midair, swinging like aromatic bells from their slender stems. The fragrance of lilac connects me to the essence of home. Vertical connections thread the past with the present and can, like *pentimenti*, penetrate the present moment.

The Persistence of Connections

Despite our Western notion of individualism and the supremacy of self, the fact is we are an amalgamation of vertical and horizontal connections that expand and contract throughout our lives. We are never free from past and present influences.

Understanding how these connections influence and relate to each other is perhaps material for an entire book, but for our purposes, know that each garden suggested in this book will be constructed around your personal experiences and requirements.

No two gardens will ever be exactly alike because each one of us brings to the creation a unique combination of experiences and history. If I suggest selecting a large rock, a pond, or a mound of earth as a center for a garden, but you are attracted to a tree stump, a gazing ball, or a sundial, by all means, use what has meaning for you.

When you are true to your own unique associations, the potential of each garden will be magnified. Unearthing your connections is your first task. A garden ultimately must speak to your soul.

Review Your Connections

1. Make a list of the vegetation you recall from your childhood with which you have a positive association. For example, you might remember an oak tree fondly because it protected you from rain as you waited for a school bus.
2. Walk outside and decide which places evoke identifiable feelings. For example, a side yard may feel protected and safe from prying eyes.
3. List the kinds of textures you like against your skin.
4. Recall aromas that evoke emotions. Do you like the sweet bouquet of gardenia or the aromatic perfume of lavender?
5. Consider the familiar sounds of nature that you like to hear. For example, the sound of a chirping cricket on a summer night or the whistle of the wind through the tree branches may be especially evocative.
6. While you may have a favorite color to wear, that color might not be your favorite to see. To help unearth your feelings about color, consider the first thought or word that comes to mind when visualizing the different colors.

Red
Yellow
Blue
Green
Magenta

Black
White

What are gardens but expressions of the self, and the self is the only true source and catalyst for change. Only within the deepest reaches of our inner being can we decipher the appropriate paths that can lead us to our heart's desires. To reach a point in our lives when our wishes reflect reality is what most of us yearn for.

BALANCE, OR YIN AND YANG

Our body strives to maintain internal equilibrium. Being out of balance implies some breakdown, some interruption of the flow of energies within, whereas being balanced furnishes us with the best chance to flourish.

There are times when we will want to create an imbalance in our environment. For Georgia O'Keeffe, a totally white room, devoid of color except her paint palette, was the catalyst for creativity. Whatever our reasons, the balance or deliberate imbalance in our environment should be considered.

A garden can galvanize a response. A winter's garden can bring in the warmth and physical freedom of summer during a time that is typically cold and constrictive.

A garden can reinforce life's experiences. Even if you are satisfied with your career and personal development, a power garden can help you sustain this feeling. In any case, a distinctive outdoor space can either enhance or preserve the status quo or increase the likelihood of attaining a sought-after goal.

A garden that speaks to our soul can restore or preserve our internal balance.

ENERGY, OR CHI

Energy is central to life. Without it we could not survive. Every moment in our lives is consumed by different energies. Some are Herculean, such as managing small children and a full-time job. And some are small, like properly ironing an article of clothing in order to be impeccably groomed. Prioritizing helps us determine the amount of energy we should invest in each goal.

Energy inspires growth, be it physical, emotional, or spiritual. Inherent in growth is change that can transform our perspective. Even if all things were the same, viewing the world from six feet off the ground is infinitely different than viewing it from three feet. Small children often change their vantage point by standing on a piece of furniture to deliver an important message. Likewise, a garden can furnish us with fresh energy by supplying us with a unique vantage point.

A special garden can help focus energy in areas that are important to you. For example, if your creativity needs encouragement, choose a fertility garden. A healing garden can be additional medicine for a chronic illness. Banish insecurities with a power garden. Each special garden creates an appropriate energy to lift, adjust, and blend with your intentions and speed you on the way toward achieving your desires.

In addition to providing an outlet for those of us who enjoy digging in the earth and watching plants grow and thrive, a special garden can be a source of inspiration. This book is devoted to helping you strengthen those areas in your life that need enhancement. These gardens are additional paths to trod when traveling toward self-fulfillment.

As a garden energizes the self, you can bring energy to a garden by attracting birds and butterflies. To be in a space that teems with life is inspiring. What athlete is not spurred on by the crowds? Life begets life. To be around living, breathing creatures that float and dance through a garden can be stimulating, as well as life-sustaining. The first step is to know which plants are likely to attract birds and butterflies.

Plants That Attract Butterflies

Butterflies are welcome guests in almost everyone's garden. Selecting plants with nectar will encourage them to visit.

Be sure to check the master plant list in the back of the book for more options.

Trees

Horse chestnut (*Aesculus*)
Madrone (*Arbutus*)
Chaste tree (*Vitex*)

Shrubs

Butterfly bush (*Buddleia*)
Wild lilac (*Ceanothus*)
Lavender (*Lavandula*)

Annuals and Perennials

Yarrow (*Achillea*)
Jupiter's beard (*Centranthus*)
Cosmos (*Cosmos*)
Delphinium (*Delphinium*)
Beardtongue (*Penstemon*)
Buttercup (*Ranunculus*)
Gloriosa daisy (*Rudbeckia*)
Sage (*Salvia*)

Plants That Attract Birds

Fruit, seeds, and flowers attract birds into your garden. However, when using fruit as your lure, you'll be sacrificing some of the visual appeal of the plant material because the birds will eat the fruit when it is most delectable.

Birds are attracted to a huge array of plants. The following are some favorites. Be sure to check the master list in the back of the book for more options.

Trees

Mimosa (*Albizia*)
Birch (*Betula*)
Crab apple (*Malus*)
Pine (*Pinus*)
Oak (*Quercus*)
Elm (*Ulmus*)

Shrubs

Manzanita (*Arctostaphylos*)
Flowering quince (*Chaenomeles*)
Dogwood (*Cornus*)
Silk tassel (*Garrya*)
Grevillea (*Grevillea*)
Firethorn (*Pyracantha*)

Perennials and Annuals

Snapdragon (*Antirrhinum*)
Lion's-tail (*Leonotis*)
Nicotiana (*Nicotiana*)
Beardtongue (*Penstemon*)
Hummingbird's trumpet (*Zauschneria*)

Vines

Trumpet vine (*Campsis*)
Clematis (*Clematis*)
Cardinal climber (*Ipomoea*)
Flame vine (*Pyrostegia*)

3

Clarity, Complexity, Mystery, and Refuge

In the best of all possible worlds, we feel compelled to explore and enjoy the outdoors. The concepts of clarity, complexity, mystery, and refuge can transform a mundane landscape into paradise. Frederick Law Olmsted, landscape designer of more than 300 parks, including Central Park in New York City, had a genius for creating spaces that elevated the concepts of parks into public sanctuaries. In addition to its almost ethereal feeling, an Olmsted setting compels us to enter, intrigues us to explore, and persuades us to remain.

We tend to think of a natural landscape as preferable; however, there are subtle and not-so-subtle differences between a natural "look" and vegetation that has been left alone. Human intervention has left its mark, to a greater or lesser degree, on all land managed by human beings. Forests provide more than wood for building; many woodlands have been managed for centuries to provide animal fodder, kindling, and thatching materials. In order to harvest these materials, the forests were stripped of thorny, tangled scrub to make foot passage possible.

An appealing walking surface unencumbered by hazards is necessary to invite us to explore. The incentive to set foot in an unfamiliar setting might simply be a path that wends its way out of sight, a clearing with logs perched by a stream's edge, or a bed of pine needles under a canopy of branches that screens the sun. In any case, unless a scene intrigues us, or unless we see a pleasing spot to rest, we will not likely enter or stay. Clarity, complexity, mystery, and refuge are notions not normally associated with gardening, yet without these ingredients we are not likely to explore and remain in even the most delightful garden.

CLARITY

Human beings need recognizable landscapes. I remember when my parents took my sister and me to the World's Fair in Brussels. At supper one evening before our nightly trek to the fair, I convinced my parents to let me add a bit of wine to my water. At fifteen, the effect of wine was swift, and in this condition my parents let my sister and me loose in the House of Mazes. The maze consisted of a series of small rooms, each with one wall of glass facing the public domain, two mirrored walls, and a fourth wall with an opening into the next room. The rooms were positioned at strange angles to each other, so there was no logic to the flow from room to room. Consequently, my sister and I traveled in circles and could not distinguish a mirrored wall from one that led into another room and ultimately out of the maze. Being the elder of the two, I was expected to find the way out, but I was completely lost in illegible space. I remember my parents' faces pressed to the glass, trying to lead us out with their pantomime gestures. We emerged after many frustrating minutes to the great relief of us all. Only diehards enter territories that are completely foreign and unknown. Most of us need clarity in order to negotiate a space easily.

In order for us to feel "at home," certain expectations need to be met. Inside our homes, we expect to find a light switch by the entrance door of a room. Likewise, we need to be able to anticipate some elements in a garden setting. The following are guidelines to consider when creating clarity for any outdoor space. Legibility communicates a common language.

1. *Create an edge.* A room needs walls that define the perimeter. Even though a garden does not have traditional walls, it needs a border to define its shape. Just as children are likely to feel better when there are rules or limits, as adults we feel better when we know where one space stops and another starts.

2. *Create pathways.* Pathways encourage use. Each garden should have a defined pathway leading to it. One house in my neighborhood does not have a defined path to the front door. My writing room overlooks the property, and I can easily see any visitor approaching this entrance. In the last ten years, I have seen no one use the front door. Instead, visitors skirt around the house to the

back where a deck extends from the back door. The deck's surface substitutes as a path; thus, it feels more appropriate as an entrance. Few approach a place without a path.

After we enter, pathways leading through a space help us negotiate the space confidently. If we are forced to circle around furniture in order to reach our bed or are blocked by a hedge to get to a special garden, we might avoid using it or become frustrated. Traveling in towns and cities can be agonizing because the roads are often obstructed with traffic. No one likes obstructed routes.

3. *Create a threshold.* A threshold is like a hug. It provides a special welcome. Stone pillars, a trellis of plants, sculpture, bells, or ceramic pots can add something familiar to an entrance to help define it and welcome those who cross it.

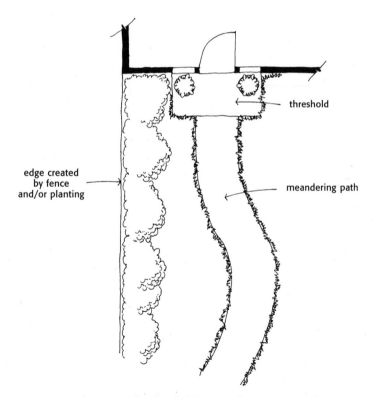

Edges, pathways, and a threshold create clarity in an outdoor area.

4. *Create a depth view.* Not being able to see where we're going is intimidating. A depth view gives us the feeling that we know enough about the terrain ahead to feel safe enough to proceed.

A jeweler once took me to visit a business in Providence, Rhode Island, that displayed antique findings and faux stones in boxes that were stacked from floor to ceiling. We felt like kids let loose in a candy store because the rooms were filled with "treasures," from shiny icons to fabulous fake gemstones. The only drawback was the narrow aisles meandering carelessly throughout the giant building. That, coupled with the lack of a depth view, made us feel claustrophobic. Evidently, I was not the only one who experienced these feelings, because on a return visit I noticed a painted yellow line on the floor of the aisles that helped clarify the exit route. Without a depth view, a space can feel uncomfortable. And when we are uneasy, we are likely to refrain from entering.

5. *Create a legible heart.* A heart is a place we feel compelled to approach. A garden needs an appropriate feature that captures our attention and draws us to it. A mound of dazzling yellow daffodils, a huge boulder, or aerating waters in a pond are examples of features that can be used as the heart of an outdoor space.

The heart helps define use. For example, the single heart of a meditation garden can be a rock or a cluster of plants. A child's garden might have two hearts, such as a vegetable patch to care for and eat from and a tented picnic table that can serve for feasting or playing. The heart is where your intentions and attention lie.

COMPLEXITY

A variety of divergent details creates complexity. Complexity lures us into a setting. Who wants to explore a featureless lawn? Complexity gives the eye a reason to explore. For example, we can scan a football field of grass in an instant, but when the players hit the field, we tend to break up the scene into many different vignettes. We rarely get bored if there is the right amount of engaging detail in a scene.

Conversely, too much complexity can be confusing. If that football field were invaded by all the people in the stands, we would have difficulty focusing on any one particular part. Too many details make an engaging scene impenetrable.

To gauge if there is enough complexity in your garden, study it to determine if you have provided a full spectrum of visual experiences. There must be a mixture of empty and full spaces, as well as a variety of colors, shapes, and sizes. All things being equal, the difference between an ordinary meal and a gourmet meal is in the seasoning. Complexity adds spice to a landscape.

MYSTERY

Mystery is not surprise; instead, it is the promise of more. Turning a corner and facing a cliff is a surprise, but turning a corner and seeing a path that fades away behind a hedge of roses is a mystery. It is an enigma that invites a solution.

Furnish a garden with something to inspire curiosity. Placing a seat close to a tree can stimulate the observation of a delicate design etched in its bark. When we are positioned to detect something not normally observed, the benefits of mystery are evoked. Mystery is a remedy for boredom.

A straight, uninterrupted route is not tempting, and a tight, serpentine path ultimately frustrates. Mystery is achieved by balancing what is known with what is anticipated.

REFUGE

Refuge supplies a welcoming setting. My Russian grandmother would greet us by asking us to sit down and make ourselves comfortable. Having a space of our own is an indispensable part of wanting to stay. No one prolongs staying in a room when all the seats are occupied.

There is no limit to the different types of objects that can provide refuge in any setting. A bent-willow chair, a huge boulder, or a log placed by a stream all invite us to stay awhile. Refuge can be implied or real. A tire swinging from a tree signals that this is a place for children, and even if you are well past the age of careening through the air in a tire, the implication can satisfy the need to experience it.

To determine if your garden has an appropriate amount of clarity, complexity, mystery, and refuge, take the following test.

TEST FOR CLARITY, COMPLEXITY, MYSTERY, AND REFUGE

Answer all questions. If appropriate, you can choose more than one answer. If there is no selection that best describes your situation, score a zero on that question.

1. Can you mentally locate all major trees within visible distance from your home?

    +2 if you can identify every major tree
    +1 if you can identify most trees
    −2 if you have forgotten to include more than three trees that are higher than the dwelling

2. Would a guest be able to predict what's in your backyard by standing on your front lawn?

    +2 if a guest would be totally surprised by what is in the backyard
    +1 if a guest would find a few surprises
    −2 if a guest could easily surmise what's in back

3. What can you see from your home's windows?

    +1 for each different view
    +1 if you can see facial expressions on a person walking on the sidewalk or street
    −1   for a view of land lacking a variety of vegetation
    −2 for each window without a view of more than eight feet

4. Do you walk around or visit the property between your dwelling and the street?

    +2 every day
    +1 every week
    −1 about once every ten days
    −2 only when you have to mow the lawn

5. Are there places to sit outside?

    +2 if there is seating in your front yard
    +2 if there is seating in your side yard
    −1 if there is no place to sit in your side yard
    −2 if there is no place to sit in your backyard

6. What do you do outside?

> +2 if you rest, read, or chat
> +2 if you rearrange items and while away the hours gardening
> +1 if you picnic
> −1 if you just mow the lawn
> −2 if you rarely go outside

7. Do you . . .

> +2 go outside to see the arrival of spring's buds or a fresh
>   snowfall or to smell the fragrance of a recent bloom?
> −1 go outside but stay on a patio or deck most of the time?
> −2 experience your yard mostly through a window and spend less
>   than twenty minutes per day outside?

Add up all the scores and arrive at one score. For example, if you have scores of 10 positive and 5 negative, your total score would be +5. Read the scoring explanation that follows to determine how you and your land rate with clarity, complexity, mystery, and refuge.

If you have scored:

−5 or lower   You are cut off from an experience of nature. Get busy and make a garden to add to the quality of your life.

−4 to +4   You are in that gray area where your landscape adds nothing to the quality of your life. A few changes could produce dramatic results.

+5 to +14   The spaces surrounding your home are compelling enough to help you benefit from their presence. With a small effort you can create an unparalleled positive experience of nature.

+15 or higher   You're off the charts and have every reason to believe that your landscaping is superb. With the addition of a special garden, your kingdom will be even more wondrous.

4

SHAPES AND
THEIR MEANINGS

△ Triangle = Fire = South
□ Square = Earth = Center
○ Round = Metal = West
≈ Wavy = Water = North
▭ Rectangle = Wood = East

The way we use words often communicates hidden meanings. Consider the expression, "the shape you're in." Shape, in this context, means the collective conditions of a life as expressed by your physical and mental condition. Could it be that shapes are aligned with deep internal feelings? According to the principles of feng shui, each shape expresses different emotions and, therefore, is preordained to benefit different areas of our lives.

Here's an example. Undulating shapes are linked to the element of water. Water will flow around pebbles, tree roots, or anything blocking its path. Sweet pea tendrils curl in the air until they find a place to attach themselves. When they do this, they are mimicking the "shape" of water. When we view curves, we are reminded on a subliminal level to bend and yield in order to achieve our goal, rather than remain fixed or struggle. Seeing wavy or curved lines facilitates the notion of winning by relinquishing control. "Go with the flow" is both literal and metaphoric.

Vertical lines suggest growth and development, like a growing tree. A triangular shape is reminiscent of a flame, and a round shape evokes the smooth surface of metal. We are influenced by what we see, and whether we are aware of it or not, we receive messages from the shapes of the things surrounding us. We should be aware of these implicit messages when we select plants for our gardens, and when planning a garden, we should not only strive for pleasing aesthetics, but also choose shapes that will convey appropriate messages.

We experience the shape of some vegetation differently throughout the year. When considering the influences of foliage, be sure to consider a plant's shape both in bloom and in its dormant state.

Shapes can imply direction, too. By orienting a garden in a particular direction we are implying an element's message. For example, a triangle, by its association with a flame, can conjure up the warmth of the south in the northern hemisphere.

△ Triangle

Triangle = Fire = South

Consider a triangle. Like a flickering flame, its shape is volatile and expresses tension, as does a love triangle or the Bermuda Triangle. When we look at fire, we know something is mutating. It is not hard to understand why triangles are aligned to the element of fire and the direction of south. On a subconscious level when looking at a triangle, we are warmed physically and emotionally.

Triangles represent heat, activity, and action. The pointed convergence of a triangle's lines is sharp and daggerlike. Its spiked shape can actually or visually pierce what it's directed toward. Triangles incite.

Ferns are wonderful examples of a trianglular fire shape. Ferns typically grow in dark, moist places, and their overall triangular shape combined with their pointed leaves balances the experience of dark and wet. Fire can light up and dry out and is a perfect counterpoint to a fern's likely site.

Choose plants with triangular leaves when you want to obliterate sadness, depression, or feelings of being overwhelmed. A triangle can spark an emotional or intellectual response and is good to use when academic pursuits are embarked upon or for occasions that benefit from ceremony.

Nature has an uncanny way of linking form with function. The evolutionary process culls each species' form to its highest and best. For example, many evergreen trees have an overall triangular shape. Evergreen trees whose branches start close to the ground, such as cedars and some pines, have the most pronounced overall triangular shape and often grow in colder climates. What a happy coincidence that their shape evokes a feeling of both warmth and action in northern or wet places where they typically grow.

Triangles with their diagonal lines send strong messages. Diagonal lines are dynamic and hard to miss. Artists know that diagonal lines are the most visually compelling. Westerners read newspapers from the top left to the bottom right or at a diagonal. We are, it seems, almost compelled to follow a diagonal line. Traditional feng shui pays so much attention to stairways in a home, in part, because their overall diagonal shape is hard to ignore.

Even if you don't select plants with triangular-shaped leaves, you can evoke the feeling of this shape by positioning plants of different heights in a triangular arrangement.

The diagonal lines in plants with triangular shapes send strong messages.

Triangles Encourage	Triangles Discourage
Tension	Peace
Fear	Restfulness
Distrust	Trust

Suggestions for Using Triangles

Power Garden: Position a triangular shape in the area of the ba-gua (octagon) that needs invigorating. (See Chapter 10 for information on the power garden. The concept of ba-gua is explained in Chapter 6.)

Meditation Garden: The shape of the trees backing the contemplation area may be triangular. (See Chapter 11.)

Lover's Garden: Consider a triangular-leafed plant as one of the symbols of male and female plants located at the threshold of the inner sanctum. (See Chapter 12.)

Healing Garden: Energize the shape of light shining down by carving out a triangular opening. (See Chapter 13.)

Child's Garden: Configure a triangle for the overall shape of the uprights at this garden's threshold. (See Chapter 14.)

Fertility Garden: If possible, place this garden on the south side of your property or near a south window. At least one set of plants should have triangular leaves or blooms. (See Chapter 15.)

Winter's Garden: The main feature should include a triangle-shaped evergreen, grouping of scrubs, or roof of a birdhouse. (See Chapter 16.)

Retirement Garden: A triangle is an appropriate shape for the top of a fence post edging the back of this garden. (See Chapter 17.)

Plants with Triangular Fire Shapes

Be sure to review the master list of plants at the end of the book for other options.

Leaves and Flowers

Iris (*Iris*)
Calla lily (*Zantedeschia*)
Bird-of-paradise (*Strelitzia*)
Belladonna lily (*Amaryllis*)

Overall Fire Shape

Birch (*Betula*)
Spruce (*Picea*)
Tulip tree (*Liriodendron*)

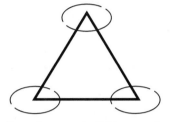

Triangles as floor plans create tight, uncomfortable spaces.

In general, a triangular shape is not a positive shape for the garden itself because the corners defined by the walls are constricted. An unused space can make us feel unproductive or useless. The tenets of feng shui suggest that if we have spaces in our lives that are not utilized, we may have talents that we're wasting. In general, don't use a triangle as an overall garden shape.

☐ SQUARE

Square = Earth = Center

It's hard to imagine that only five hundred years ago the earth was considered flat. Now, when we think of our planet, we immediately think of a sphere. With photographs from space used to sell anything from software products to soap, few of us conjure up any shape but round when evoking the image of the earth.

However, if we were asked to verbalize the feeling of earth, we would not be comfortable describing being earthbound as existing on a round surface that rotates. The equal-sided square, the most stable of shapes, when it is squat and thick, elicits the feeling of being planted on earth.

Although very few leaves or blooms appear to be square, the overall shape of a plant or a bed can be experienced as a safe, secure square earth shape. Windows through which we view a vista are more often than not rectangles, but outside we are not constrained by a manufacturer's dimensions. We can sculpt openings in our liv-

The stability of a square can be
perceived in a plant's overall shape.

ing garden walls into any shape we want, including the secure, safe earth square.

Squares Encourage	Squares Discourage
Groundedness	Nervousness
Stability	Venture-taking
Security	Individuality
	Conflict

Squares are good shapes for gardens for young children who need confidence while away from the nest. Square planting beds can help those entering medical facilities feel more stable and secure. Persons suffering from multiple sclerosis or other conditions that interfere with the ability to negotiate easily through space may benefit from square-shaped designs, especially near inclines. Use square vignettes within any garden to root and anchor.

Suggestions for Using Squares

Power Garden: A deck or a raised mound of earth from which a power garden is viewed can be a square. (See Chapter 10.)

Meditation Garden: The bed that houses the focal point may be a safe square shape. (See Chapter 11.)

Lover's Garden: A square is a good shape for the second chamber in this garden. (See Chapter 12.)

Healing Garden: The stable square is appropriate for the overall shape of this garden. (See Chapter 13.)

Child's Garden: As the overall shape of this garden, the square conveys security. (See Chapter 14.)

Fertility Garden: At least one set of plants should be as tall as they are wide. (See Chapter 15.)

Winter's Garden: A square can be the shape of the window through which we view this garden. (See Chapter 16.)

Retirement Garden: The pathway adjoining a retirement garden should be more square than rectangular. (See Chapter 17.)

Plants with Square Earth Shapes

Be sure to review the master list of plants at the end of the book for more options.

Blooms

California poppy (*Eschscholzia*)
Rockrose (*Cistus*)
Rose (*Rosa*) some varieties

Low or Earth-Shaped

Wormwood (*Artemisia*)
Boxwood (*Buxus*)
Juniper (*Juniperus*) some varieties

○ ROUND

Round = Metal = West

Precious metals are associated with refinement, grace, and density, and most metal is thought of as resistant and intense. Metals are formed when pressure reduces and compresses the minerals in the earth. Like metal, we physically and mentally roll up into a ball when pressure is exerted on us. It is natural to recoil when confronted by a flying object such as an intangible bellow of complaints flung our way.

From ancient to modern cultures, certain metals have long represented wealth, status, and achievement. For centuries, gold with
its deep, warm luster and silver with its cool, reflective shine have
been used to create statues, medallions, adornments, and currency.
The process of obtaining these metals required arduous, often dangerous, labor. Likewise, the processes of converting the raw materials into valued objects required extreme temperatures and
dangerous working conditions. As the fires heated the metals, so
too, the acquisition of precious metals fired the human imagination.

Metal is associated with a round shape. When it is heated to a
certain temperature, the molten metal will form round beads.
Roundness, too, has been associated with quality and status. Circles, or round shapes, have been used for rings, crowns, and even
Olympic medallions.

When American wine producers decided to change wine's traditional cylindrical bottle to a square paper container, they quickly
discovered the public would purchase expensive wine only if it was
enhanced by the sophisticated refinement of a round bottle. The
people who chose to buy wine in square containers didn't typically
look for estate and vintage years but wanted stability of pricing and
taste.

A dome is a metal shape. The use of a dome for capitol buildings may be the result of the architects' intuitive knowledge of the
association of shape with activity. Nothing can be tucked away or
hidden inside a dome. The shape implies considering all aspects that
are at the core of all wise and lasting decisions. However, like a
rolling ball, nothing ever stays the same, and while we need to
examine each moment, we should accept the fact that all things
come to an end.

Last, the element of metal is associated with endings. And like
the sun's descent in the west, metal can glide us to another hori-
zon. Metal also can be associated with the colors white or gray
because nature drains the color from our hair and from animals' fur
and the luster from plants as the end of life's cycle approaches.

Round Encourages	Round Discourages
Control	Freedom
Erudition	Humbleness
Enlightenment	Dissipation
Acceptance of endings	Autonomy

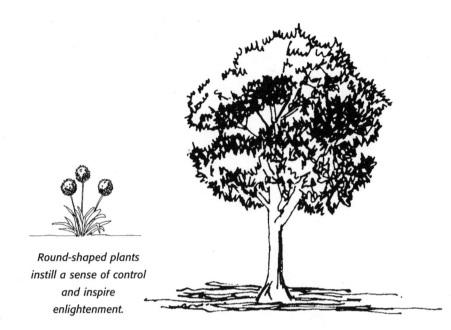

*Round-shaped plants
instill a sense of control
and inspire
enlightenment.*

Suggestions for Using Round Shapes

Power Garden: Use rounded or dome shapes in the section of the ba-gua where learning or new information needs to be integrated. (See Chapter 10.)

Meditation Garden: The rounded figure eight is appropriate for the overall shape of this garden. (See Chapter 11.)

Lover's Garden: The shape of the circle of two in the inner sanctum implies both equality and inner wisdom and the liberation from the desire to be entirely autonomous. (See Chapter 12.)

Healing Garden: Create a round opening in the ceiling through which light shines in. (See Chapter 13.)

Child's Garden: Round shapes can be a tire swing, a log to climb, or a tunnel for a hiding space. (See Chapter 14.)

Fertility Garden: Include at least one set of plants with round leaves or blooms. (See Chapter 15.)

Winter's Garden: Incorporate round shapes in the focal point of this garden. (See Chapter 16.)

Retirement Garden: Select round blooms for this garden. (See Chapter 17.)

Plants with Round/Metal Shapes

Be sure to check the master plant list in the back of the book for more options.

Blooms

Globe thistle (*Echinops*)
Chive (*Allium*)
Hydrangea (*Hydrangea*)

Dome-Shaped and/or Metallic Silver-Gray

Wormwood (*Artemisia*)
Lavender cotton (*Santolina*)
Lamb's ear (*Stachys*)

≈ Wavy or Curved

Wavy = Water = North

Water wends its way around obstacles to ultimately find its destination. Curved lines, like waves, imply the ability to yield without compromising the goal.

Water takes on the color of its surroundings. Seawater can appear azure blue, like the color of the tropical sky. A pond's water can have a greenish cast caused by the algae growing in it. The shallow waters of a riverbed can look muddy, reflecting the color of the earth in its channel. By using plants with black, turquoise, or blue blooms or plants with curved lines, we can evoke the essence of water.

The essence of water is evoked in plants with curved or wavy lines.

We are buoyed up by water, but we can also feel enveloped by its power. In a positive way, water or gently moving curved lines can help us relax. Conversely, dramatic twisting lines challenge us in the same way that wind or vastly uneven land disturbs water and creates a range of action from ripples to whitewater rapids.

Curved-shaped flower beds can be used in a child's garden to encourage the mind to wander and be unencumbered by restraints. For someone who feels vulnerable and is trying to regain a sense of power, dominant curved shapes can exacerbate feelings of insecurity. After all, our human shape cannot back up snugly to a curved wall, nor can we feel emotionally backed up with curved edges or borders.

Curved Shapes Can Augment	Curved Shapes Can Deter
Gestation and germination	Free movement
Strength from nonaction	Loneliness
Feeling overwhelmed	Nervousness
Peace of mind	Frenetic energy
Optimism	Autocratic behavior
Relaxation	
Acceptance	

Suggestions for Using Curves

Power Garden: Use curved plants in any of the ba-gua areas that would benefit from optimism. (See Chapter 10.)

Meditation Garden: Curves are a choice for a shape inside the focal area and the garden's overall shape (figure-eight shaped). (See Chapter 11.)

Lover's Garden: Curves are suitable for the paths leading to and within this garden. (See Chapter 12.)

Healing Garden: Enjoy the curved lines that vines make as they grow up a trellised wall. (See Chapter 13.)

Child's Garden: Create curved beds for vegetables and flowers. (See Chapter 14.)

Fertility Garden: Wavy lines add interest to the center of this garden. At least one set of plants should have curved, wavy blooms. (See Chapter 15.)

Winter's Garden: Curved lines can contribute to a sense of acceptance with optimism. (See Chapter 16.)

Retirement Garden: Peace of mind evoked by a curved edge of a raised bed is perfect for this garden. (See Chapter 17.)

Plants with Wavy/Curved Water Shapes

Be sure to check the master plant list in the back of the book for other options.

Blooms

Globe thistle (*Echinops*)
Hydrangea (*Hydrangea*)
Iris (*Iris*)

Curved-Shaped Foliage

Honeysuckle (*Lonicera*)
Chinese wisteria (*Wisteria*)
Windflower (*Anemone*)
Plantain lily (*Hosta*)

☐ RECTANGLE

Rectangle = Wood = East

Plants, like human beings, stretch upward until they reach maturity. Thus, a rectangular shape, which implies movement, is a symbol for growth. When viewing rectangular shapes, we can be inspired to accept new ideas and leap toward change. The element of wood, by its association with growth, is a symbol not only of the shape of a rectangle, but also of its spirit of expansion and change.

In a similar way, the direction of east or the rising sun is associated with growth and change, for a day's renewal holds the promise of transformation. Many of us are refreshed more than physically by the opportunity of beginning anew each day.

Both vertical and horizontal rectangles connote personal growth.

Rectangles can be seen vertically or horizontally, and although both orientations imply growth and change, we experience them slightly differently. A vertical rectangle is the overall shape of tree trunks and flower stems. When we look at vegetation, we see, in more cases than not, that plants have a vertical stem from which other growth develops.

A horizontal rectangle connotes growth also, but in an oblique way. In the same way that we learn to understand more and more words after initially learning the alphabet, lateral growth implies an increased capacity to explore the known, as opposed to seeking entirely new information. Lateral awareness gives us the ability to consider the feelings of others and to be able to mediate and accommodate existing circumstances. A horizontal rectangle, by its direction, entreats us to deal with the here and now.

Since nothing stays the same, we need to reinforce change as a common experience in life. Without the ability to change, we decline physically, mentally, and emotionally.

Vertical Rectangles Encourage

Growth
Change
Dreams
Power

Vertical Rectangles Discourage

Patience
Laziness
Feeling overwhelmed
Tenaciousness

Horizontal Rectangles Encourage

Conquering
Mediation
Persistence

Horizontal Rectangles Discourage

Stagnation
Self-centeredness
Complacency

Suggestions for Using Rectangular Shapes

Power Garden: The vantage point from which you view a power garden can be rectangular. (See Chapter 10.)

Meditation Garden: Position a rectangular shape behind the seating area. (See Chapter 11.)

Lover's Garden: Use a rectangular shape for the second threshold leading into the inner chamber of a lover's garden. (See Chapter 12.)

Healing Garden: The shape of this garden's walls can be rectangular to promote positive growth. (See Chapter 13.)

Child's Garden: One or more edges should be vertical rectangular shapes, such as a wood fence or a stand of trees. (See Chapter 14.)

Fertility Garden: The overall shape can be rectangular, whether it is a container or a bed of soil. At least one set of plants should feature more stalks than blooms. (See Chapter 15.)

Winter's Garden: Trees stripped bare of foliage reveal rectangular shapes. (See Chapter 16.)

Retirement Garden: The raised bed can be a horizontal rectangle. (See Chapter 17.)

Plants with Rectangular/Wood Shapes

Consult the master plant list at the back of the book for other options.

Overall Rectangular Shapes

Holly (*Ilex*)
Dogwood (*Cornus*)
Cypress (*Cupressus*) some varieties

WEEPING SHAPES

To add to our discussion of shapes, weeping shapes are not directly associated with an element or a cardinal point. Nevertheless, they represent a close connection with nature and natural forces.

The force of gravity pulls things toward the earth. Weeping shapes suggest a gentle flow that appears to reconnect with the earth. We draw strength from a renewed connection with mother earth.

Given this positive connection to the earth, why do we use the term *weeping*? Do we feel that having to bend is sad? Are we suggesting that to give in is distressing? Perhaps we associate sagging lines with an aging body and draining energy. Not defying gravity suggests giving in. Whatever the wellspring from which these ideas emerge, a weeping shape can be perceived as either positive or negative, depending on the context.

Weeping Shapes Can Augment	**Weeping Shapes Can Deter**
Connection	Egotism
Memories	Letting go
Feeling satisfied	Envy
Magic	Stodginess

Suggestions for Using Weeping Shapes

Power Garden: Use weeping shapes in the section of the ba-gua where jealousy or isolation is felt. (See Chapter 10.)

Meditation Garden: Weeping shapes are not appropriate in this garden. (See Chapter 11.)

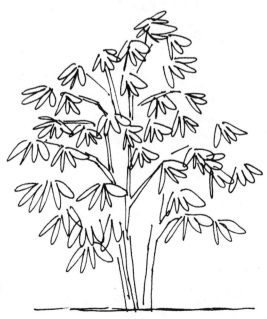

Weeping shapes represent a renewed connection with the earth.

Lover's Garden: Use weeping shapes for the edging vegetation surrounding the circle of two. (See Chapter 12.)

Healing Garden: Blooms hanging off the vines that grow up the walls can conjure the up the magic for recovery. (See Chapter 13.)

Child's Garden: Sprinkle weeping flowers in the patch of plantings, especially if more than one child typically plays there. (See Chapter 14.)

Fertility Garden: Weeping plants can be placed at the edges of the container. (See Chapter 15.)

Winter's Garden: Weeping shapes are not used in a winter's garden. (See Chapter 16.)

Retirement Garden: Use weeping shapes to edge the front of this garden and help feel satisfied with the way things are. (See Chapter 17.)

Plants with Weeping Shapes

Be sure to review the master plant list at the back of the book for more options.

Trees

Willow (*Salix*)
Deodar cedar (*Cedrus*)
Willow myrtle (*Agonis*)

Shrubs and Perennials

Chinese lantern (*Abutilon*)
Silk tassel (*Garrya*)
Honeysuckle (*Lonicera*)
Fuchsia (*Fuchsia*)

5

COLOR

I was astonished when my parents brought home our first color television. Even though our old TV was black and white, I had mentally colored all the programs I watched. The actual colors came as a rude shock to me because they did not quite match the colors I had imagined. Lucille Ball's red hair was perhaps the most surprising. I hadn't thought it was a cross between a popsicle and a VFW's crepe-paper poppy. Color is so pervasive an experience, it seems we imagine it even when it's not there.

Faber Birren, in his groundbreaking book, *Color & Human Response*, describes how a few people can identify color without seeing it. They sense a color by touch and can identify colors accurately and repeatedly under controlled conditions. Describing the feel of colors, one of the book's subjects explained that light blue felt smoothest; yellow, slippery; and red, green, and dark blue, sticky. She said some colors repelled her from going toward them, while others seemed to invite tactile exploration. Colors appear to have a variety of textures, not dissimilar to the skin of different fruits.

Although colors are seen and perhaps "felt" in the same way, we experience them differently, depending on our cultural point of view. Take, for example, the color orange, which is not a popular color in Western culture. Orange is a color of fusion. While it actually blends red and yellow, it connotes the union of ideas or actions. Since Westerners value individuality over conformity, the notion of melding is not popular. Cultural values exhort us to be ourselves, to stand out in a crowd, or to be all that we can be, clichés notwithstanding. We love to be unique. On the other hand, Buddhist monks wear saffron robes because their goal is to reach fusion with spirit. The color orange expresses a monk's goals perfectly.

Studies have been conducted on other species to determine the effect of color. Although fish cannot see color, studies show that they generally either shun red or strongly prefer it. In other words, they react to red in a measurable way.

Why have we assigned pink as the color for baby girls? The Environmental Health and Light Research Institute conducted an experiment on marine life reproduction. Researchers observed that if a fish tank was flooded with pinkish light, female births outnumbered male births by four to one. There is some quality in pink that supports being female. We don't know what it is, but someday we may.

All colors elicit responses, and knowing what each color evokes is important when selecting blooming plants for a garden. Before we delve into the specifics of individual colors and responses to them, let me caution you about usage.

As eating too much food, even if it's healthful and nutritious, can cause gastrointestinal distress, too much color in a confined area can provoke a negative reaction. While the reaction to color is immediate and intense, if one is overexposed to a color, the opposite outcome can be realized. For example, the color red can stimulate. If you would benefit from stimulation after a hard day at work, then consider planting red flowers by the entrance to your home. Consider, though, how you would feel if, after entering your home, the walls were also a bright red. Too much red elicits anxiety. Remember that when using color to evoke an emotional response, more is not necessarily better.

The color with which we surround ourselves invades our consciousness with special meanings. Consider the color's message before selecting it for a plant or flower. Here is a chart that can guide you in the selection process.

Color Chart

Red	Ignites, stimulates
Lavender	Allows us to be free from cravings
Magenta	Sparks higher mental, emotional, and spiritual processes

Purple	Reinforces supremacy, links to an elevated state
Orange	Inspires fusion
Adobe	Reflects connection
Saffron	Kindles love
Terra cotta	Strengthens security
Yellow	Clarifies
Sand	Crystallizes investigation
Tan	Reduces individualism
Gold	Expresses abundance
Green	Explores expansion and growth and also promotes tranquility
Light green	Evokes wistfulness and relief
Lime	Awakens the spirit
Verdigris	Deepens commitment
Blue	Expresses self-esteem and mystery
Powder blue	Invites contemplation
Turquoise	Deepens ecstasy
Cobalt	Connects to a higher purpose

RED

Reds tend to stimulate us, perhaps because they produce measurable changes in our blood pressure and breathing. Red is composed of long wavelengths that seem to jump out at us. Many of us have experienced sitting in a stadium and viewing a crowd across the playing field. Our eyes gravitate toward the people wearing red jackets, scarves, and hats. Looking at red is akin to entering a room filled with aerobic dancers. As we observe everyone moving around, we tend to feel stimulated by all the action. Who hasn't taken a surreptitious leap in the air after watching a particularly energetic ensemble of dancers? Use red to give rise to feelings, conversation, and activity.

Looking at red increases our blood pressure, pulse, and respiration. Red also stimulates our brain and our skin. A red jacket feels warmer than a white jacket. Red revs us up. But beware, like an athlete collapsing at the end of a marathon run, too much red can wear us out.

Red Encourages	Red Discourages
Energy	Contemplation
Excitement	Focus on mental activities
Feeling warm	Feeling morose

Suggestions for Using Red

Power Garden: Fire-engine red connotes power in the future area of the ba-gua. (See Chapter 10 for information on the power garden. The concept of ba-gua is explained in Chapter 6.)

Meditation Garden: Use reddish tones in stepping-stones leading to this garden or for occasional blooms along the pathway's edge. (See Chapter 11.)

Lover's Garden: Scatter red flowers in pairs throughout. (See Chapter 12.)

Healing Garden: Hang the special object with a red ribbon from the garden's ceiling. (See Chapter 13.)

Child's Garden: Use red blooms for a patch of vegetation. (See Chapter 14.)

Fertility Garden: Do not use red in this garden. (See Chapter 15.)

Winter's Garden: Place a plant with reddish/orange bark or a red object near the focal point. (See Chapter 16.)

Retirement Garden: Incorporate flowers with deep red blooms that contrast sharply with their leaves. (See Chapter 17.)

Red Blooming Plants

Be sure to check the color plant chart in the back of the book for other options.

SPRING

Annuals	Perennials
Stock (*Matthiola*)	Jupiter's beard (*Centranthus*)
Pansy (*Viola*)	Beardtongue (*Penstemon*)
Sweet pea (*Lathyrus*)	Coralbells (*Heuchera*)

SUMMER

Annuals	Perennials
Aster (*Aster*)	Peruvian lily (*Alstroemeria*)
Verbena (*Verbena*)	Bleeding heart (*Dicentra*)
Petunia (*Petunia*)	False spirea (*Astilbe*)

AUTUMN

Annuals	Perennials
Begonia (*Begonia*)	Windflower (*Anemone*)
Dahlia (*Dahlia*)	Chrysanthemum
Phlox (*Phlox*)	(*Chrysanthemum*)
	Blanketflower (*Gaillardia*)

WINTER

Annuals	Perennials
Snapdragon (*Antirrhinum*)	Primrose (*Primula*)
Stock (*Matthiola*)	
Pansy (*Viola*)	

ORANGE

Mixing yellow with red helps the energy become clearer. If uncovering emotions or facilitating communication with others is sought, adding yellow to red can help.

In the 1950s and 1960s, when television was becoming a family staple, orange became a popular decorating color. My theory is that this color was an unconscious attempt to keep a family connected through conversation, instead of through shared interest in watching a program. Orange promotes conversation.

Orange, the color of fusion, can be used in classrooms, negotiation chambers, courtrooms, and shared areas. This is the color to use when compromising is a benefit.

Orange Encourages	Orange Discourages
Fusion	Individuality
Conversation	Isolation
Spirituality	Insecurity

Suggestions for Using Orange

Power Garden: Orange is appropriate for the relationships area of the ba-gua. (See Chapter 10.)

Meditation Garden: Plant orange blooms around the focus of this garden. (See Chapter 11.)

Lover's Garden: Use orange blooms for the vines growing on the threshold of the second chamber. (See Chapter 12.)

Healing Garden: Orange is an appropriate color for an object used for seating. (See Chapter 13.)

Child's Garden: Either the seat of the swing or an object close to the swing can be orange. (See Chapter 14.)

Fertility Garden: The second closest blooms to the center should be orange. (See Chapter 15.)

Winter's Garden: Place a tree or bush with a reddish/orange bark near the focal point. (See Chapter 16.)

Retirement Garden: Orange is suitable as the edge color (brick walls) or in flowers close to the edge. (See Chapter 17.)

Orange Blooming Plants

Be sure to check the color plant chart in the back of the book for more options.

SPRING

Annuals	Perennials
Pot marigold (*Calendula*)	Peruvian lily (*Alstroemeria*)
Pansy (*Viola*)	Daylily (*Hemerocallis*)
Snapdragon (*Antirrhinum*)	Peony (*Paeonia*)

SUMMER

Annuals	Perennials
Begonia (*Begonia*)	Canna (*Canna*)
Zinnia (*Zinnia*)	Iris (*Iris*)
Chrysanthemum (*Chrysanthemum*)	Black-eyed Susan (*Rudbeckia*)

AUTUMN

Annuals	Perennials
Dahlia (*Dahlia*)	Golden Marguerite (*Anthemis*)

Pot marigold (*Calendula*)   Pink (*Dianthus*)
Marigold (*Tagetes*)   Blanketflower (*Gaillardia*)

Winter

Annuals   **Perennials**

Snapdragon (*Antirrhinum*)   Primrose (*Primula*)
Iceland poppy (*Papaver*)
Pansy (*Viola*)

Yellow

Although we normally think of red as the most vibrant and easy to see, the color yellow increases an object's visibility. Safety experts choose yellow for the line in the middle of a road because it's easier to see. Not only does yellow brighten, but also whatever image it colors becomes effortless to pick out.

The macula lutea is a small yellowish area lying slightly off the center of the retina that constitutes the region of maximum clarity in our eye. It is not an accident that its color matches its properties. I tell students of feng shui to refer to nature when seeking answers. Just as our sun produces light for us to see, yellow is the color producing maximum illumination. Yellow represents light, both actually and metaphorically.

Yellow Encourages   **Yellow Discourages**

Clarity   Egocentricity
Abundance   Isolation
Mental illumination   Laziness

Suggestions for Using Yellow

Power Garden: Yellow is a good choice for the wisdom area of the ba-gua. (See Chapter 10.)

Meditation Garden: For a few plantings surrounding the focus of this garden, yellow is an excellent selection. (See Chapter 11.)

Lover's Garden: Yellowish blooms can enhance the circle of two. (See Chapter 12.)

Healing Garden: A pine or yellowish wood can be used for building the braces for the walls and ceiling. (See Chapter 13.)

Child's Garden: Incorporate an electric light at the threshold or a globe painted yellow. Yellow can be the color of tall grasses and blooms in the flower garden. (See Chapter 14.)

Fertility Garden: Yellow blooms should be the second closest to the edge. (See Chapter 15.)

Winter's Garden: A yellow electric light can shine on the garden after sundown. (See Chapter 16.)

Retirement Garden: Use yellow profusely throughout. (See Chapter 17.)

Yellow Blooming Plants

Be sure to check the color plant chart in the back of the book for other options.

SPRING

Annuals	**Perennials**
Iceland poppy (*Papaver*)	Columbine (*Aquilegia*)
Pansy (*Viola*)	Iris (*Iris*)
	Peony (*Paeonia*)

SUMMER

Annuals	**Perennials**
Dahlia (*Dahlia*)	Peruvian lily (*Alstroemeria*)
Strawflower (*Helichrysum*)	Daylily (*Hemerocallis*)
Zinnia (*Zinnia*)	
Primrose (*Primula*)	

AUTUMN

Annuals	**Perennials**
Marigold (*Tagetes*)	Black-eyed Susan
Dahlia (*Dahlia*)	(*Rudbeckia*)
Sunflower (*Helianthus*)	Chrysanthemum
	(*Chrysanthemum*)
	Blanketflower (*Gaillardia*)

WINTER

Annuals	**Perennials**
Primrose (*Primula*)	Euryops (*Euryops*)
Snapdragon (*Antirrhinum*)	

Iceland poppy (*Papaver*)
Pansy (*Viola*)

GREEN

Relaxation and change are inherent qualities of green. Arise from a bed of soft summer grass and discover how your spirit and body are altered. Relaxation replenishes our capacity for growth. We breathe deeply when surrounded by green.

Although it is almost impossible to step outdoors without seeing green, we should be aware of this color's flip side. Because we are swept away by nature's overwhelming presence, green can diminish our individuality. We can be engulfed by green and lose our mechanisms of control of self. Green is not necessarily good underfoot when stability is compromised or when growth needs to be checked.

Green Encourages	Green Discourages
Growth	Internal focus
Feeling tranquil	Control
Awakening	Generosity

Suggestions for Using Green

Power Garden: Place green in the descendants area of the bagua. (See Chapter 10.)

Meditation Garden: The seated area's backdrop should be green. (See Chapter 11.)

Lover's Garden: Green should appear profusely on the walls and floors of the threshold of both chambers. (See Chapter 12.)

Healing Garden: Green is a suitable dominant color for the walls. (See Chapter 13.)

Child's Garden: Use green as one color in the threshold. (See Chapter 14.)

Fertility Garden: The leaves of all the plants in this garden, especially the ones used to weep over the edges, should be green. (See Chapter 15.)

Winter's Garden: At least one evergreen tree or bush should be part of the entire scene. (See Chapter 16.)

Retirement Garden: Incorporate green throughout the plantings, especially at the farthest edge. (See Chapter 17.)

Green Blooming Plants

Be sure to check the color plant chart in the back of the book for other options.

SPRING

Perennials

Spurge (*Euphorbia*)
Hellebore (*Helleborus*)
Coralbells (*Heuchera*)
Iris (*Iris*)

SUMMER

Annuals

Bells of Ireland (*Moluccella*)
Coleus (*Coleus*)
Mignonette (*Reseda*)

Perennials

Coralbells (*Heuchera*)
Iris (*Iris*)

AUTUMN

Annuals

Flowering cabbage (*Brassica*)
Zinnia (*Zinnia*)

WINTER

Annuals

Flowering cabbage (*Brassica*)

Perennials

Hellebore (*Helleborus*)

BLUE

Blue lowers our rate of breathing, blood pressure, and temperature. Blue is used for meditation and is the color associated with turning inward. Even our blood is blue inside our body and only turns red when it's exposed to the air. Realizing this makes it easier for us to understand why blue is thought of as a color that expresses self.

Ask any clothing manufacturer; men buy blue clothing more frequently than any other color. Blue is considered the favorite color of American men. Males in our culture have traditionally been taught to regard themselves as dominant and powerful; the color blue supports this. Many meditation tapes suggest conjuring an image of a blue room to begin the meditative process. Blue, the quintessential color of self and meditative states, must be used cautiously because too much blue can cause depression. We even refer to feeling despondent as "feeling blue."

Not many flowers are blue. By definition, a flower is the choicest part of a plant that is concerned with production of the fruit or seed. Reproduction, in part, depends on the flower that attracts animals and insects through color to disseminate the plant's seeds. The need to attract other species by the visual or vibratory messages of color would preclude selecting a color that promotes isolation. Therefore, blue plants are likely to attract less activity, and so they became uncommon. Use blue for inward journeys and to cement self-esteem.

Blue Encourages	**Blue Discourages**
Slowing down	Conversation
Self-esteem	Optimism
Ecstasy	Eating
Relaxation	Feeling energized
Spirituality	Insecurity

Suggestions for Using Blue

Power Garden: Blue is a good choice to use in the self area of the ba-gua. (See Chapter 10.)

Meditation Garden: Use blue as the color for the heart of this garden. (See Chapter 11.)

Lover's Garden: For vines on the threshold of the first chamber, blue is an appropriate color. (See Chapter 12.)

Healing Garden: A choice for blooms on the trellis includes blue. (See Chapter 13.)

Child's Garden: Blooms near hiding areas can be shades of blue. (See Chapter 14.)

Fertility Garden: A blue water feature enhances this garden. (See Chapter 15.)

Winter's Garden: Use blue sparingly, if at all, in this garden. (See Chapter 16.)

Retirement Garden: Blue is a possible hue for pathway material. (See Chapter 17.)

Blue Blooming Plants

Be sure to check the color plant chart in the back of the book for more options.

Spring

Annuals

Bachelor's button (*Centaurea*)
Forget-me-not (*Myosotis*)
Pansy (*Viola*)

Perennials

Columbine (*Aquilegia*)
Iris (*Iris*)
Lupine (*Lupinus*)

Summer

Annuals

Ageratum (*Ageratum*)
Aster (*Aster*)
Lobelia (*Lobelia*)

Perennials

Lily of the Nile (*Agapanthus*)
Delphinium (*Delphinium*)
Verbena (*Verbena*)

Autumn

Annuals

Lobelia (*Lobelia*)
Morning glory (*Ipomoea*)

Perennials

Aster (*Aster*)
Salvia (*Salvia*)
Pincushion flower (*Scabiosa*)

Winter

Annuals

Cineraria (*Senecio*)
Sweet pea (*Lathyrus*)
Pansy (*Viola*)
Violet (*Viola*)

Perennials

Primrose (*Primula*)

Although color can affect sentiment, it is also personal. Without analyzing why, we all have preferences. When in doubt, choose colors with your heart.

6

THE BA-GUA

Where you sit in a classroom can often express your feelings about school. Most teachers will attest to the fact that students who choose to sit in the front of the classroom are often more attentive. Feng shui suggests that locations are imbued with specific characteristics. Where a person is positioned in any space can affect his or her experience. Likewise, the position of an object influences the people within its space.

The Chinese divide the ba-gua, an octagonal shape, into nine sections. The sections are positioned in relationship to the entrance. Each area is imbued with a meaning. The pyramid school has interpreted an area's message in line with more contemporary Western concepts.

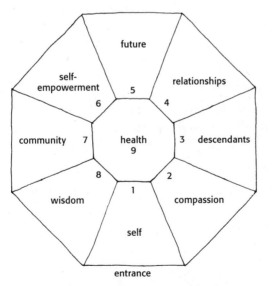

A modern interpretation of the ancient ba-gua.

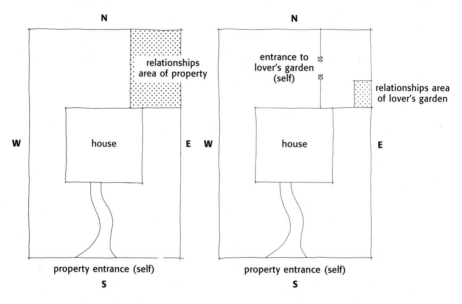

In terms of outdoor spaces, the ba-gua can be used to determine the positions either for the entire property or for each individual garden. For example, you may want to position the lover's garden in the relationships area of the property but have the entrance to the garden facing east, thus causing the garden's ba-gua locations to be different from those of the entire property.

SUGGESTIONS FOR EACH BA-GUA SECTION

Self-Fulfillment Areas

Areas Closest to the Entrance

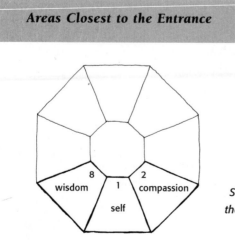

Self-fulfillment areas of the ba-gua are closest to the entrance.

Our childhood experiences often color how we react in the future. The habits we develop and how we interact with the world of ideas and people are learned early in our lifetime. Similarly, the areas closest to the entrance of a space influence important areas in our lives. In the ba-gua, these are the self-fulfillment areas: self, wisdom, and compassion.

Self-Fulfillment Area 1

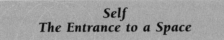

Self
The Entrance to a Space

You are at the epicenter of all experiences. Therefore, where you enter a space is critical to how you experience it. While the familiar can be comforting, the exotic can be exciting. Normally, the space to enter precludes plantings, except for the area surrounding the threshold. What to plant adjacent to the entry door is highly personal and cannot be prescribed. Look in Chapter 7, "Plants as Symbols," and select a message that speaks to your soul. Be sure that you really want what you ask for, because you are likely to get it.

Suggestions for Plants in the Self Area

Carpet bugle for power to succeed
Azalea for moderation
Jasmine for confidence
Morning glory for optimism
Juniper for trusting your own judgment
Fuchsia for courage
Marigold for releasing jealousy

Self-Fulfillment Area 8

Wisdom
Left of Entrance

The area to the left of the entrance is reserved for wisdom, a resource used to steer us prudently through life. Wisdom is a rudder constructed of insight and knowledge that can help us deal with joy, tragedy, and all the continuum of life's experiences.

Emphasize this position to assist feeding wisdom. Yellow, the color of clarity, and round, the shape of mental acumen, can be useful in this area.

Suggestions for Plants in the Wisdom Area

Clematis for clarity of the mind
Sunrose for emotional wisdom
Yellow azalea for generating new ideas
Daffodil for profusion of ideas
Sage for pure thoughts

Self-Fulfillment Area 2

Compassion
Right of Entrance

Traditional feng shui calls this area the "helpful people corner," hoping that the world will stand ready to assist us in achieving what we desire for ourselves.

The pyramid school advocates the notion that what we put forth for others will be returned; therefore, the right side, which is the side most people feel comfortable using, can be put to use to support whoever enters. When unfamiliar with a place, we often pause to brace or ready ourselves before entering. By placing something familiar and soothing or something to lean against in that area, we show our concern for others. When we make others feel comfortable, they will want to do the same for us.

Sturdy plants, fragrant blossoms, or edible berries are some of the vegetation we can plant in the compassion corner. In this area, wavy, or water, shapes express depth of feelings for others.

Suggestions for Plants in the Compassion Area

Raspberries for giving
Apple tree for releasing negativity
Date palm for lasting friendships
Lilac for sensuality
Gardenia for indulging
Japanese maple to protect values

Power Areas

Areas Farthest from the Entrance

As biological creatures, we feel safest when we are farthest away from an entrance because distance gives us time to react. This harks

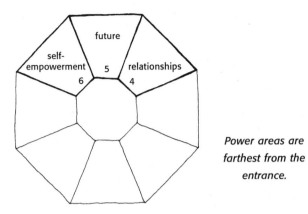

Power areas are farthest from the entrance.

back to our cave-dwelling days when we needed to have space separating us from dangerous predators that might enter our domain. Being situated at the greatest distance from an entrance helps us feel more secure and powerful. In the ba-gua, the power areas are self-empowerment, future, and relationships.

Power Area 6

Self-Empowerment
Back Left Wall

The area on the left-hand side of the power wall resonates with personal growth, self-improvement, and self-empowerment, in part because it combines the power with the left side. The left hand, the nondominant side for the majority of the human population, is the side that we are less likely to turn toward. Since we have to concentrate to rotate to our left, we are more likely to be focused when turning in that direction, and this inward focus helps us achieve power.

Plants with purple, red, or magenta blooms can align us with a higher consciousness and can assist us in transforming desires into reality. Rounded leaves and bushes trimmed to a rounded shape will help us be sharp and focused for the journey.

Suggestions for Plants in the Self-Empowerment Area

Peony for accepting ourselves as we are now
Dahlia for challenging ourselves
Foxglove for maintaining equanimity
Hibiscus for reaching out
Edelweiss for daring to scale heights

Power Area 5

Future
Center of Back Wall

The area in the middle of the back wall is associated with the future. Whether we wish on a star or try to visualize a goal, the future is experienced as directly ahead and slightly out of reach. The future can be represented by the colors red, blue, or yellow, depending upon what emotions are best suited to help actualize goals. For example, if you want to use your higher consciousness as a guide, plant purple blooms.

The triangle, or fire shape, is dynamic and well suited to the future area. Triangular leaves can be the flame that keeps the goals energized.

Suggestions for Plants in the Future Area

Violets to maintain the status quo
Clematis for a brighter future
Iris for creating a new reality
Crocus for changes augmenting happiness
Chrysanthemum to remember the past
Buttercup for clarity of vision

Power Area 4

Relationships
Back Right Wall

The right-hand side farthest from the entrance links us to relationships. Since most human beings are right-handed, cultures typically use right-handed gestures for greeting. The entire right side is therefore associated with communication with others.

The designers of Disney's projects know that the public will feel less anxious waiting in long lines if they start by turning the public to the right. When an area of communication is needed, choose the far right side of any space to help facilitate the flow of conversation, ideas, and feelings.

Planting at least two of each species with orange blooms will express a commitment to communication, and selecting low-growing plants, rather than vines, for the relationships area will keep you grounded and down-to-earth while working toward solidifying your commitment to another person.

Suggestions for Plants in the Relationships Area

Welsh poppy for optimism
Marigold for selfless love
Rose for true love
Clover to put fate in your hands

Support Areas

The Center

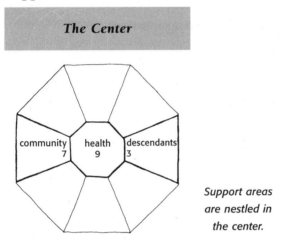

*Support areas
are nestled in
the center.*

Nature safeguards our vital organs by positioning them in the center of our body. In this position they are protected as well as accessible to other areas of the body. The central positions in the ba-gua are occupied by community, health, and descendants (the major support systems that sustain us). Be sure to select hardy plants for this central position. Annuals are not the best choice for the central position of a garden unless they produce seeds that can be easily sowed in the next season.

Support Area 7

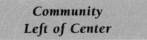

Community
Left of Center

In order to thrive, we require that an ever-broadening support system be in place. Today self-sufficiency is rare, and it is difficult for us to survive without strong social and political networks. We depend on the talents of others and the structure of the community to safeguard our lives and lifestyles.

Like water, the experience of community runs deep, and its value is not always apparent. Even though most of our own body is composed of water, our liquid content is mainly unfelt and unseen. A water feature—the color black or curved, wavy lines—acknowledges the depth of our need for a strong community.

Suggestions for Plants in the Community Area

Barberry to help see reality
Black tulip to honor the special qualities in all
Tree trunks to preserve our connection with the past
'Molly Sanderson' pansy to solidify community spirit
Mint for growth

Support Area 9

Health
Center

Any experience in life can be influenced by how we feel. Optimal health of our physical self, mental condition, and spiritual well-being are the linchpins that hold together our essence. If we do not thrive physically, mentally, and spiritually, we are likely to feel short-changed.

Plant climbing vines in gardens' centers to visually and viscerally express healthy growth. If climbing vines are not appropriate for the climate and soil conditions, then sow plants of varying sizes adjacent to each other to contrast the varying degrees of growth.

Suggestions for Plants in the Health Area

Bougainvillea for flourishing
Clematis for change with growth
Gladiolus for overall well-being
Verbena to restore balance
Rhododendron for ongoing well-being
Tulip for restoring health

Support Area 3

Descendants
Right of Center

The desire to sire offspring is the single most powerful drive for any species. We procreate mainly to preserve ourselves. Perhaps that's why sexual appetites are so strong when we are of childbearing age and less important when we are not.

Today, more so than in the past, many adults choose not to have children. There remains, however, the need to influence the future. Therefore, descendants, besides genetic offspring, can be the product of our thoughts and actions. Descendants are the ticket to our passage into future generations. Moreover, our influences extend beyond the capacity to sire or affect others. They also result from our creativity and imagination. Whether we are carried into the future by people, ideas, or deeds, one thing is for sure: we are motivated to influence what will be.

Strength, growth, and consistency are the allies of survival. Plants that resonate with these traits are ideally suited to the descendants area.

Suggestions for Plants in the Descendants Area

Pine for immortality
Aloe to heal past transgressions
Queen Anne's lace for survival
Chive for absorbing negativity
Yarrow to eliminate unwanted conditions
Shasta daisy for endurance
Texas blue star for self-fulfillment
Jack-in-the-pulpit to honor the unique
Butterfly weed to attract helpers
Echinacea to heal the scars
Plantain lily for proliferation

Whether you apply this information to an individual garden or to the property as a whole, planting with intention will increase the chances that the benefits will manifest themselves. Utilizing plants to express your intention is tantamount to having a full-time ombudsman assisting you to reach your heart's desires.

7

PLANTS AS SYMBOLS

We express ourselves through our personalities and, in the best-case scenario, our expressed self will interact with others in an optimum way. Plants, like people, have personalities, and over time they have become associated with them.

Natural selection equips a species with what it needs to endure. Attracting bees to its flower may be the best method for a particular plant to ensure its survival. A small, low, colorful species that originated in a region of tall, pale grasses may exist only because of its bright pigment. In many cases the appearance is a result of changes that assisted continuation for that species.

The essence of a plant often emerges as its symbol. The date palm, for example, grows erect and straight most of the time. Perhaps that's why it can be considered as a symbol of triumph over adversity. Its leaves have been used as a symbol for Christians on Palm Sunday.

It is hardly odd that a plant's healing properties would become the basis for its inherent value or meaning. Plants are the source for countless medicinal remedies. In fact, their curative properties are many times the basis for synthetic drugs. Digitalis, a medication used to assist in healing heart problems, is derived from foxglove. The vapors from eucalyptus leaves can clear the sinuses and have been associated with helping people crystallize or clarify their thoughts.

Most often the symbolic meaning of a plant will be a composite of many factors and can vary from culture to culture. In any case, should there be a discrepancy between the universal meaning and a local one, it is better to accept the indigenous interpretation. Although live oaks grow in many places in Florida, and have no special meaning attached to them, here in my town, where they grow almost to the ocean's edge, there is a strong belief that live oaks are a symbol of good luck. This belief evolved here because no devastating hurricane has come ashore in recent history, and live oaks, which are slow-growing trees, are symbols that we live in a protected area. Traditional folklore hands down a legend of birch trees as talismans for successful marriages, perhaps because they bend rather than break in a strong wind. Folklore often converts real attributes into symbols.

Once you have become familiar with the symbolic meanings of plants, you will never look at or create a garden in quite the same way. Just as our houses have rooms for different activities, so should a garden supply the background for a variety of needs. Surround yourself with appropriate inspirational messages.

The list of plants and their meanings is a contemporary interpretation that links a plant's physical traits with ancient folklore, medicinal properties, and contemporary Western culture's point of view.

Plants and Their Meanings

Ajuga bronze	Infuses power to succeed
Aloe	Soothes and heals
Apple tree	You may be tempted to quit or go your own way.
Ash	Strength through flexibility
Azalea	All is waiting for those who are moderate.
Bamboo	Longevity
Barberry	Provides clarity
Basil	Sincere good wishes are endearing.
Bay laurel	Protectors
Beech tree	Flexibility is the root of strength.
Belladonna	Sometimes silence is the best policy.
Birch	Flexibility will help withstand pressures.
Black tulip	Helps you honor unique qualities
Bougainvillea	Triumph over adversity

Buttercup	Clarity in deed
Butterfly weed	Attracts helpers
Carnation	Graciousness without pretension
Cedar tree	Cleansing and preserving
Chive	Absorbs negativity
Chrysanthemum	Honor the past.
Clematis	Clarity of the mind
Clover	Fate is in your hands.
Columbine	Pursue your dreams, but don't be foolish.
Crocus	The newness of love stirs us.
Daffodil	Pay attention to those around you.
Dahlia	To challenge yourself
Daisy	Simplicity is the essence of profound thought.
Dandelion	Synchronize your life with nature's rhythms.
Date palm	Survival
Echinacea	To heal your scars
Edelweiss	Dare to scale heights and achieve results.
Eucalyptus	Clarifies emotional and physical receptiveness
Evergreens	Be consistent, and love will be yours.
Forget-me-not	Focus
Foxglove	Helps maintain equanimity
Fuchsia	Courage to communicate your needs
Gardenia	Find the courage to speak the truth.
Geranium	Triumph through persistence
Gladiolus	Lifts spirit and restores well-being
Heather	Seek to discover yourself.
Hibiscus	The path is more important than the rewards.

Holly	Think before taking action.
Honeysuckle	Impetus to change is lodged in the here and now.
Impatiens	Do not be impatient.
Iris	Creativity will bear fruits of contentment.
Ivy	Don't spread yourself too thin.
Jack-in-the-pulpit	Honors uniqueness
Japanese maple	Protects values
Jasmine	Trust yourself.
Juniper	Consciously decide to accept or reject advice.
Jupiter's beard	Be compassionate, and compassion will be returned.
Lavender	Detachment is a virtue.
Lemon	Awakens and unlocks
Lilac	Return to clarity
Lily	Listen to the innocent, for they often lead the way.
Lily of the valley	Be undaunted in combating and conquering.
Lotus	Peel away until the truth is revealed.
Magnolia	Physical beauty is fleeting.
Maple	Make waves; capture attention.
Marigold	Don't be consumed by jealousy.
Mimosa	Don't be thin-skinned.
Mint	Easy victories are not necessarily lasting.
Mistletoe	Wards off evil spirits
'Molly Sanderson' pansy	Solidifies community spirit
Morning glory	Vitality of beginnings
Mushroom	Survives darkness
Myrtle	Love is the highest and best goal.
Narcissus	Don't let ego interfere with wisdom.

Nasturtium	Vitality in the face of challenges
Oak leaves	Be brave.
Oak tree	You will survive.
Palm tree	Victory
Pansy	Reach deep inside for thoughtful answers.
Parsley	Intensity of purpose
Peony	Regard the significance of the moment.
Pine	Retains equanimity and fosters understanding
Pink carnation	Remembrance of the past can infuse the present with meaning.
Plantain lily	Augments proliferation
Pomegranate	Maturity brings rewards.
Queen Anne's lace	Fortifies survival
Raspberry	Fosters learning to share
Rhododendron	Living in harmony will produce ongoing well-being.
Rose	Love what you do or else don't do it.
Rosemary	Remember me.
Sage	Purify your thoughts and actions.
Shasta daisy	Endurance
Snapdragon	Don't ever assume.
Sunflower	Being best is fleeting; being happy is forever.
Sunrose	Helps reach emotional wisdom
Tansy (wild)	Wage battle.
Texas blue star	Personal fulfillment
Thorn apple	Be wary of charm; it may be deceitful.
Thyme	Find courage and energy for your heart's desires.
Tiger lily	Be prideful carefully.
Tree trunks	Nuances can support.

Tulip	Turning adversity into victory
Verbena	Tenacity triumphs.
Vines	Distinguish between being absorbed and being strangled.
Violet	Faithfulness is your companion.
Wallflower	Don't be afraid to be an individual.
Welsh poppy	Releases optimism
Willow	Freedom is to be sought at any price.
Yarrow	Change should be instituted subtly.
Zinnia	Absence

FLOWERS OF THE MONTH

There are charts advising which flowers are associated with each month. Moreover, many cultures have flowers associated with different seasons and months. Whether these lists are based on commercialism or fanciful notions that certain flowers can express the essence of a time of year is less important than the fun that comes from knowing which flower to hold aloft as its symbol for a given month.

Because feng shui is a tradition of China and because our political and cultural heritage comes in great measure from the English, it might be interesting to know what flowers are associated with the different months in these countries. However, as with all pyramid school notions, nothing remains the same when viewed in a new situation. Our knowledge of flowers is influenced by our soils, our mixed heritage, and our varied climatic conditions. Therefore, the American feng shui calendar of flowers differs from the others. With great respect for the past and reverence for the here and now, I offer you the following feng shui calendars of flowers.

English Flowers of the Month

January:	Snowdrop
February:	Primrose
March:	Violet

April:	Daisy
May:	Hawthorn
June:	Honeysuckle
July:	Water lily
August:	Poppy
September:	Morning glory
October:	Hops
November:	Chrysanthemum
December:	Holly

Chinese Flowers of the Month

January:	Plum blossom
February:	Peach blossom
March:	Tree peony
April:	Cherry blossom
May:	Magnolia
June:	Pomegranate
July:	Lotus flower
August:	Pear blossom
September:	Mallow blossom
October:	Chrysanthemum
November:	Gardenia
December:	Poppy

American Feng Shui Flowers of the Month

January:	Gladiolus
February:	Daisy
March:	Crocus
April:	Tulip
May:	Pansy
June:	Butterfly bush
July:	Hydrangea
August:	Pink rose
September:	Buttercup
October:	Chrysanthemum
November:	Marigold
December:	Poinsettia

Whether you choose to consciously memorize the meanings or emotionally absorb their essences, let the language of plants guide and advise you.

8

A Few Sensible Things

Bigger Is Not Always Better

My mother always said my eyes were bigger than my stomach whenever I piled my dinner plate to capacity and then couldn't consume even half of it. A surefire way to guarantee not completing a project is to make a grander schedule than it is possible to complete within a reasonable period of time. When planning a garden, think about details, not size.

It is better to finish a small special garden and use it sooner than to wait to complete a huge one. If you do choose to have a prodigious garden and know that it will take time to complete, I suggest making a small indoor model in a planter until the larger one is ready. It is better to nurture yourself with a few smaller meals each day, rather than a gargantuan meal once a week; likewise, when creating a garden, it is far better to enjoy the benefits of less, more frequently.

The selection of plants often hinges on emotional instead of rational factors. Seed catalogues are my nemesis. How can I not want the luscious blooms shown in vibrant colors on their pages? It would be a Herculean feat for me to provide the proper care and duplicate the conditions that allowed those plants to grow to their full potential. I may be in the right region for a certain plant, but the composition of my soil, the exact precipitation during critical periods, and the optimal sunlight or shade may vary from the ideal. Sometimes I am lucky, but more often than not, the blooms in my garden don't match the pictures in the catalogue. Don't expect them to, but be joyous if it happens.

When bringing home a plant from the local nursery, you should be prepared for the discrepancy between how it looked there and how it looks in your garden. In a garden it may look puny, compared with how it appeared in the nursery, because there the plant benefited by being raised in a pot and clustered with others. When planted in your garden, its proportions shrink, like a catalogue-bought diamond ring. When purchasing, ask yourself if the size of the plant would be appropriate if it were a foot shorter or narrower.

WHO WANTS TO BE A REALIST?

Those of us who subscribe to gardening magazines or receive gardening catalogues often dream impossible dreams. In researching this book, I became enamored with gardening experts such as Julie Moir Messervy and Roy Lancaster, who design gardens far beyond the wildest capacity of us ordinary folks. However, many of you are like I am, juggling careers, family, and a host of other interests and gardening for love as well as relaxation. Whether I am mulching my vegetable patch or growing a philodendron on a stone embankment, I often look for labor- and time-saving ways to cover the ground. Yes, I look with envy at my neighbor's gardens with delicate flowers growing hardy under the Florida sun, but I know that she spends quite a substantial number of hours every week caring for the gardens and amending conditions so that these plants can thrive. I simply don't have time, and if you don't either, let's be realistic. Plant what you can care for!

Xeriscaping is a growing trend in many water-conscious areas. Simply put, Xeriscaping is growing only indigenous plant life. Instead of mowed green lawns, a xeriscaped front lawn might be filled with local wildflowers. Today the owners of the mansions in Palm Springs, California, are eschewing imported grass and landscaping with cactus and shrubs that grow naturally in a hot dry climate. If you want to try Xeriscaping, just be advised that indigenous plants must go through a full year (all seasons) before they can survive on their own. A year's investment can garner a lifetime of results!

Unlike the inhabitants of Palm Springs, I often think there is water, water everywhere, except when my plants need it! Living close to the Atlantic Ocean gives me the feeling that I live with an abundance of water. However, when choosing a plant for my garden, I look for plants that can stand to be without frequent watering. It's not that it doesn't rain frequently in Florida, it is just that the searing sun parches the earth quickly. Understanding a plant's need for water is important in the overall scheme. Ask yourself if you want to water your garden daily, weekly, or never, and choose plants accordingly. Naturally, mulching will help keep soil moist and optimize local rainfall.

Intention is usually the best part of planning. Years ago, I was sitting at our dinner table situated on a side lanai, when I noticed poison ivy growing up a live oak tree. Ah, I thought, I'll get my snippers, cut the vine at the root, and pull the roots out of the earth. Piece of cake, not more than a few minutes' work. Five days later, when I still found myself dwelling on how I could cut down the poison ivy, I realized that I had better put a plan into action. I decided to establish a routine and select a convenient time of day to stroll around the property. I combined an evening walk with checking up on my gardens. With my garden shears tucked in a pocket, I can either remedy problems or return home with freshly cut flowers. Once a routine is in place, you will find yourself ful-filling a feng shui adage that says it's lucky to visit all areas of a home and property each day.

Convenience of access is an important feature in planning a gar-den. If you need to slow down and relax more often, don't tuck a special garden in a place you're unlikely to visit regularly. Be sure each garden is accessible and easy to reach. Pathways and proxim-ity will draw you to a garden.

The Plant That Ate the World

One of my all-time favorite movies is a spoof called *Little Shop of Horrors,* which is roughly based on a story about a plant that con-sumed everything in sight. Funny and poignant, this story satirizes the "what-if" scenario of a plant going out of control.

Unfortunately, this scenario is often not far from the truth. Many times stores will sell plants because they are easy to grow. The owners are more interested in satisfying their customers than in long-term garden management. They know that it feels good to see plants thrive and multiply. However, what grows quickly and eas-ily can also grow out of control and take over an entire garden. A plant that covers one area quickly will not likely stop there.

I learned my lesson from mint plants. Reading that mint plants by an entrance door can keep flies from crossing the threshold, I quickly planted mint on both sides of my studio door because I keep it ajar all summer. Now, years later, I am sick and tired of pulling mint plants out of the way so that other plants can live. Be careful not to plant vegetation that will naturalize (spread on its own) and dominate a garden.

ASK AN EXPERT

I know it's easy to jump out of the car at a local nursery and ask a salesperson for advice. Wouldn't it be agreeable to thrust the list of plants for a particular garden under the salesperson's nose and find out if the nursery has exactly what you want? Well, I hate to be a bearer of ill tidings, but if the nursery doesn't have the plants on your list, you may have to wait until a local garden center can order exactly what you want. Soil conditions, rainfall, and shade or sunlight are crucial to your specific location. Your first job is to develop a master plan and locate the plants that are best suited to your area.

A local or county agricultural extension center, a college, a garden club, or a professional landscape service can also give good advice. These organizations are not dependent on plant sales for survival. When you need to find out which plant satisfies your specific requirements, engage the advice of experts. It is likely to save countless hours of toil, prevent disappointing results, and save your hard-earned money. Ask first.

THE PLANT THAT ATE THE TOXINS

Many of the special gardens, such as the fertility garden, can be created indoors, where our living areas may be tainted by insidious toxins. Hats off to Christopher Hallowell, Baruch College, New York City, who along with other scientists, is studying how plants can eat common airborne pollutants. We can employ nature to do the handiwork of rather expensive air purifiers, as well as add to the aesthetics of our homes and gardens. Here are common plants to consider if your air needs cleaning up.

Plants That Eat Formaldehyde

Formaldehyde is used in many carpet glues and furniture made from pressed woods. Check the labels.

Boston fern (*Nephrolepis exaltata* 'Bostoniensis')
Chrysanthemum (*Chrysanthemum*)

Gerbera (*Gerbera Jamesonii*)
Dwarf date palm (*Phoenix roebelenii*)
Bamboo palm (*Chamaedorea erumpens*)

Plants That Eat Xylene

Xylene is a solvent used in paints and varnishes. Check the labels.

Areca palm (*Chrysalidocarpus lutescens*)
Dwarf date palm (*Phoenix roebelenii*)
Dumb cane (*Dieffenbachia maculata*)
Dragon tree (*Dracaena draco*)

Plants That Eat Ammonia

Ammonia is found in many cleaning supplies. Check the labels.

Lady palm (*Rhapis excelsa*)
Lilyturf (*Liriope spicata*)
Flamingo lily (*Anthurium Andraeanum*)
Chrysanthemum (*Chrysanthemum*)

Plants That Eat Benzene

Benzene is a flammable liquid found in solvents and cleaning fluids. Check the labels.

Gerbera (*Gerbera Jamesonii*)
Chrysanthemum (*Chrysanthemum*)
English ivy (*Hedera Helix*)
Snake plant (*Sansevieria trifasciata*)
Dracaena (*Dracaena deremensis* 'Warneckii')

General Poison Eaters

If you are unsure of which toxins are polluting your air, a plant that eats more than one toxin may be just what the doctor ordered.

Peace lily (*Spathiphyllum*): ammonia, benzene, formaldehyde, xylene
Flamingo lily (*Anthurium Andraeanum*): ammonia, formaldehyde, xylene
Weeping fig (*Ficus benjamina*): ammonia, formaldehyde, xylene
Tulip (*Tulipa*): ammonia, formaldehyde, xylene
English ivy (*Hedera Helix*): ammonia, benzene, xylene

If you rent or own home furnishings, carpets, and paints that exhale toxins into your living space, the next plant you buy may save your life.

Animal-Resistant Plants

Although our lives are enriched by the presence of animals, we all hate to see the fruits of our efforts consumed by wildlife.

When selecting varieties of plants, factor in the local wildlife, and choose plants that the animals don't seem to like. Check with a garden or agricultural extension center or a professional in your area to ascertain those plants that seem to be animal resistant. In general, plants with thorns or fuzzy textures are usually eschewed by wildlife.

Part II

SPECIAL GARDENS— GARDENS OF THE SOUL

9

THE GARDENS

In the same way that our houses have rooms for different activities, a garden can supply settings for a variety of needs. Many properties have an assortment of indoor and outdoor niches and areas to accommodate different moods, activities, and people. A patch of tall sunflowers grown to provide a healthful snack can be used to shield a healing garden. Perhaps a grouping of fat pines would be an exquisite location to protect a child's garden. Or an herb garden can be considered an activity room in a retirement garden.

The different gardens discussed in each chapter provide a framework to which you can add your own special touches. Some gardens can be nestled into existing landscape and need very little effort to spring them to life. Some will be conceived in your mind and will be born as startling new additions to your property. Their value to you will be measured in part by how their expression alters your life.

If you live in an apartment, don't despair. All of the special gardens can be represented in miniature throughout your living space and can provide similar benefits. Intention is the first ingredient to garner on the road toward a goal; the intention adds value to your life just as much as the actual garden.

Each chapter is structured as though you were building the special garden from scratch. With a keen eye you will find many of the necessary ingredients provided by nature's gifted presence. Perhaps the perfect place to tuck a meditation garden is a remote side yard. A maple, palm, or pine tree in your backyard could be a perfect support for the back wall of a lover's garden. Look around and find natural attributes on the land that can be integrated into each garden.

Start the planning process by selecting a location and determining an appropriate size. Make it manageable! Each garden will have walls, doors, and windows, although we will refer to them as edges, thresholds, and piercings. The edges of your garden, like the walls of a building, can be solid or punctuated by windows and doors. Trees, trellises, fences, or plants can frame a clear view, as a window does, or like a solid wall, they can obscure what is beyond. Branches laden with leaves or vines growing up the supports of trellises can supply us with an outdoor ceiling.

The pathways leading to each garden are as important as the garden itself. Dorothy and her pals in *The Wizard of Oz* walked down a yellow brick road to the land of Oz, which according to the principles of feng shui was the perfect color and shape for this pathway to adventure and learning. Yellow, the color of wisdom, led to a place where the seekers expected enlightenment. The rectangular shape, which resonates with the spirit of growth, and the material of the brick, which is earth, grounded this high-spirited bunch as they journeyed to adventure. Thus Dorothy walked on wisdom as she grew in understanding, while being supported. The pathway prepared her for her destination. Likewise, the pathway you create can prepare you and your visitors for a passage into a new experience.

As you plan a garden and the rooms within, select vegetation for its suitability and ability to thrive in your area. Remember that national chain stores often distribute plants based on their best buy, not on considerations of the local soil or climate. If you are not familiar with a plant, ask an expert for advice before you spend money to purchase it and energy to plant it. Second, consider the characteristics of the vegetation. The shape, color, texture, and fragrance of plants carry implied messages. For example, a birch tree, which is thought of as a talisman for a successful marriage, bends rather than breaks in a strong wind. The presence of a slender young birch tree in a lover's garden can suggest flexibility.

Vegetation many times contains benefits that are not apparent to the eye. Some plants attract birds and butterflies; therefore, they add sound and movement to a garden scene. A still landscape is a dead one, and adding plants that bring life and movement to a garden is clearly desirable.

Any path to happiness is paved with the effort spent. The more energy expended, the more the rewards will be deeply appreciated. A garden gives us the opportunity to be distanced from our current mental baggage. As you become increasingly involved in planning and creating your garden, you will likely pull meaningful epiphanies from within. As a garden is nourished, so are our life's intentions.

GARDENS THAT REFLECT THE SELF

All the gardens in this book are both for your enjoyment and to assist you with specific areas of your life. By selecting a garden, you acknowledge an outdoor area that needs enhancing. Jump in and choose one to improve. Install the garden and harvest the results. Start small and think big.

Whether it's in the way you dress or the way you landscape your home, what you choose reflects who you are. My mother, for example, is known for her grand style in her contemporary home furnishings, her sophisticated wardrobe, and the exotic rock garden of my childhood home. This garden was our public statement of style. It wasn't by accident that there were exotic plants and vines, plus a dwarf dogwood tree that startled the neighborhood with pink taffeta blossoms every spring.

Many people in my mother's generation centered their lives around conventional wisdoms rather than the expression of their own needs. Today we are fortunate to live in a world that doesn't seem to thwart individual uniqueness as was the case in the recent past. Deciding what to plant and where to place it can express our lifestyle and needs. We no longer have to conform to grass etiquette and can eliminate the lawn mower from our lives.

If the spirit of intention is met, it does not matter if every detail is painstakingly precise. I remember when I was spreading my mental tentacles over the world hoping to lure a literary agent to help me find a publisher for my feng shui books. Although I didn't have time to satisfy the requirements of either a power or fertility garden, I did have time to put two flowers in a vase and place them at the bottom of the stairs leading to my office. Two flowers represented finding an agent who could duplicate my enthusiasm (see Chapter 15 on the fertility garden), and placing this arrangement in a prominent place infused me with the power to continue until I found the right person (see Chapter 10 on the power garden). Apparently, the intention—not the details—was enough because Regula Noetzli, literary agent extraordinaire, appeared in my life.

10

POWER GARDEN

Endowment

Authority

Strength

It is not by accident that castles were perched atop hills. For a castle's inhabitants, unencumbered views awakened a feeling of authority. Thrones were often elevated to endow royalty with authority and power. Even when thrones were floor level, the subjects were required to kneel. Height imbues a person with power. Perhaps, in part, this harks back to childhood when almost everything in the world, by virtue of size, seemed bigger and more powerful than we were.

The tallest buildings in cities divulge what a culture holds in esteem. In medieval Europe, the grandest buildings were normally churches and castles. In contemporary cities, buildings that house businesses capture the number one position: New York has its World Trade Center; Chicago, its Sears Tower; and San Francisco, its Transamerica Pyramid. These buildings tower over structures intended for education, religion, and government. The height of a commercial building expresses the power and authority of the enterprise within.

When we think of gardens, however, the terms *power* and *authority* are probably not the first to come to mind. Nonetheless, when we observe a garden from a lofty perch, we are in a naturally dominant position. According to the principles of feng shui, our surroundings influence how we feel. When we are positioned "above it all," the position infuses us with a feeling of power.

A power garden is designed to transfer energy to an individual and to help the individual recognize the kernel of power that is lodged inside. If you are experiencing frustrations and roadblocks that obstruct your personal goals, install a power garden to claim your right to succeed. To experience invincibility and unobstructed freedom to travel on life's highest and best path is the single most important value of a power garden. Position this garden in a prominent place, one that is likely to be seen daily.

A prominent position for a power garden might be below a balcony, deck, or flight of stairs. It is not necessary to sit and observe this garden, as long as you pass it frequently. If you do not have the topography or deck to support an elevated view, simply position this garden outside a frequently used exit door. Be creative; there are many locations to choose from if you approach this choice with an open mind.

SPARKS MENTAL, EMOTIONAL, AND SPIRITUAL PROCESSES

REINFORCES SUPREMACY

KINDLES LOVE

STRENGTHENS SECURITY

TURNS US INWARD

EXPRESSES ABUNDANCE

AWAKENS SPIRIT

DEEPENS COMMITMENT

DEEPENS ECSTACY

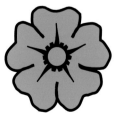

CONNECTS TO HIGHER PURPOSE

IGNITES

RELEASES FROM
INTENSE EMOTION

INSPIRES FUSION

REFLECTS CONNECTION

CLARIFIES

HELPS INVESTIGATION

EXPRESSES EXPANSION

INSPIRES NOSTALGIA

EXPRESSES SELF-ESTEEM

INVITES CONTEMPLATION

The orderly gardens of Versailles expressed the power of French royalty. These tremendously expensive creations could only be underwritten by those with the resources to hire adequate laborers. By investing in the maintenance of your power garden, you will be displaying not only the power of the dollar, but also the power of the self, because this garden, more than the others, requires time and energy to maintain.

On another level, who isn't sustained by an orderly, immaculate space? Opening my kitchen's utensil drawer and rummaging through a jumble of small gadgets until I retrieved a carrot peeler or a paring knife aggravated me until I finally bought a drawer organizer. Predictability and neatness can be a soothing ingredient for contentment. Viewing a controlled, cared-for garden nourishes and empowers us. Positioning ourselves in a commanding place can grant us self-confidence.

PLACEMENT

A power garden needs two areas—one for the planted garden and one for a place to view it. For the power garden to be successful, the vantage point needs to be considered carefully. For viewing an outdoor power garden, the vantage point could be a balcony or a mound of earth. For an indoor garden, it could simply be a comfortable, high stool. Consider the vantage point as carefully as you consider the elements of the garden.

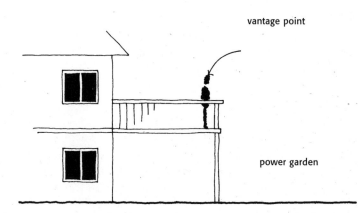

The vantage point is as important as the garden itself.

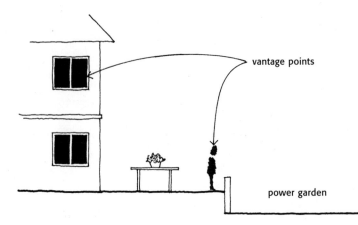

Suggestions for Vantage Points

A mound or rise of earth
A deck or balcony
An upstairs window
A chair next to a ceramic pot on the floor
The top of a flight of steps
A chair or stool

DESIGN

An important characteristic of a power garden is order. Feeling effective includes creating intention for the different areas in our lives. Visual serenity can be a springboard to action; consequently a power garden must be groomed in an orderly way. Disorder muddles our processes, but resolution is assisted by clarity. Design your passage through life as confidently and carefully as you design and maintain your power garden.

Another characteristic of a power garden is its ceremonial appearance. Repetition, uniformity, and order are important elements that enhance this characteristic. However, to achieve a formal look, you must invest time and labor in maintaining the garden. Unless you have the resources of a French king, I suggest that you select slow-growing plants to avoid intense labor and to maintain a trimmed, neat appearance.

SHAPE AND EDGES

The shape of the power garden is an octagon, which represents the ba-gua (see Chapter 6). Each area of the ba-gua defines a different area of our life. Acknowledging these different areas helps bring into focus the parts that, when fulfilled, contribute to a satisfying life.

A friend of mine recently lost three-fourths of her life's savings in a bad business deal. Since this represented her security for retirement, the news could have wreaked havoc with her whole life. However, I helped her install a power garden, and she was able to see that her security was invested in much more than just finances. By looking at all areas of her life, she was able to put in perspective this one event. Creating a visual context for life's major areas can help us see the whole accurately.

To retain the clearly defined areas of the power garden, the plants edging each area of the ba-gua can be the same throughout. By selecting an edging that works well as an underplanting, the power garden assumes a consistency that will serve it well. (Underplantings are traditionally low-growing materials underneath the

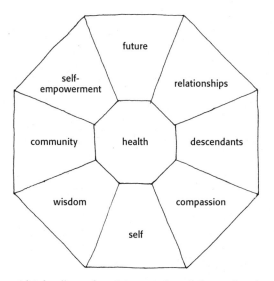

Pyramid School's modern interpretation of the ancient ba-gua.

show plants.) The edging and underplanting material should be low-growing and uniform to frame and highlight the centers of the nine areas.

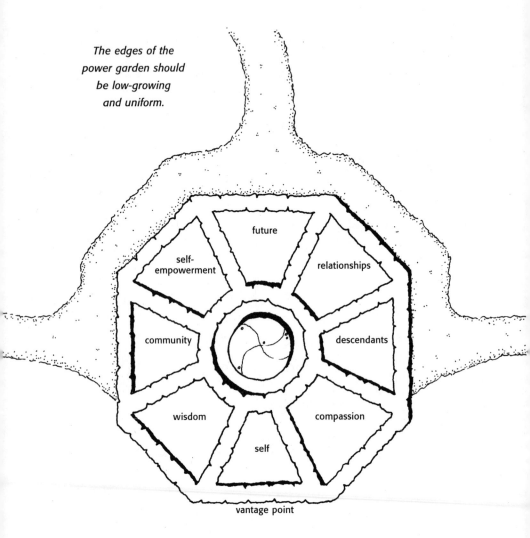

The edges of the power garden should be low-growing and uniform.

future

self-empowerment

relationships

community

descendants

wisdom

compassion

self

vantage point

Suggestions for Edging Plants

Boxwood varieties
Santolina varieties
Euonymous varieties

Pathways

Like spokes on a wheel, create at least three footpaths to a power garden. Traditional feng shui tells us that paths should be widest at the sidewalk or road to welcome those who visit. The opposite is true for the paths to the power garden. The intention of this garden is not to invite the outside world to come in; instead, the intention is to strengthen you and fill you with power and confidence, which you will take with you as you return to the outside world. By widening the path at the juncture of the garden itself, instead of when the path meets an exit road, the emphasis shifts to taking the spirit of the garden away with you as you exit actually or mentally.

Suggestions for Pathway Materials

Precast or natural stepping-stones
Decomposed granite
Gravel
Bark chips

The Heart, or Focus, of the Garden

The main focus of a power garden is the self area. The center of this garden represents mental, physical, and spiritual health. Like a heart in a body, the heart of the garden is important for the optimal functioning of all other parts. For the center, select a cherished blossom that goes through permutations. By having a view of change, we are reminded that to hold on to power, we need to be sensitive to current conditions and to be prepared for change.

For those who live in cooler climates, a permanent object such as an outdoor sculpture, a sundial, or a gazing ball can be the center. In cold climates a dwarf conifer or juniper can provide a sculptural shape under a winter's snow.

Colors

In the other sections of the ba-gua, use plants with colors that are relevant and meaningful for your life. Here is a list of suggestions for colors that express positive emotional connections. You can choose plants whose foliage approximates these colors to gain the described results. For more plentiful choices, refer to chapters 6 and 7. Also, be sure to check with your local agricultural extension center, garden club, or landscape professional for the suitability and possible varieties of vegetation.

Color Choices for Each Section of the Ba-Gua

Self-empowerment: violet or deep red
Future: fire-engine red or purple
Relationships: black, pink, or salmon
Descendants: white, toffee, or silver
Compassion: pink, ivory, or rose
Self: blue, gray, green, or terra cotta
Wisdom: yellow or gold
Community: tangerine or saffron
Health: magenta

Plant Selections

The different sections will be visually held together by the under-plantings, which could be the same as the material used for the interior pathways, or you can surround each section with uniform edging material to give an overall feeling of continuity to the different areas of the garden.

Choose a plant or an object to express the intention of each section of the ba-gua. For example, in the relationships section, two flags could express the union of two people in marriage. Like the flags, each marriage partner moves independently, but when the partners stand together in one area, they are influenced by the same elements of wind, sun, and rain. (See Chapter 6 for ample selections for each area. See Chapter 7 for lists of plants and their meanings.)

Whether you walk through your power garden or choose to view it from on high, creating it gives you an opportunity to consider the different aspects of life. Know that thoughtful, caring intention is the first footprint in a trail that leads toward success. Let the intention of a power garden steel your resolve to surround your life with the fruits of self-empowerment because the rewards of self-empowerment are laced with contentment.

11

MEDITATION GARDEN

Peace

Focus

Protection

Stillness

There are times when only a journey inward will reveal the correct path. Meditation is reflection that can bring deep personal peace and understanding. Through meditation, we can embark on an inner journey to foster positive change. Often when we contemplate, realizations float to the surface of our consciousness, giving us alternative paths and choices. Meditation uncovers feelings that can influence our reactions to life. With consistent practice, meditation allows us to be in the moment without angst because it soothes our internal chatter. Meditation grants us contentment.

The heart of a meditation garden should draw us like a magnet. The focal point of this garden should be one feature that stands out from the surrounding landscape. It should provide us with a focus on which to concentrate. Like a motionless object on a stage of moving dancers, a rock that is surrounded by slender grasses swaying with the slightest breeze will command our attention.

In addition, the focus of a meditation garden should suggest the unknown. The act of meditating helps us unearth what is not consciously apparent. Water, a boulder, or the naked earth are essences to consider for the center. A distinctive feature that incorporates one or more of these elements can serve as a focus for meditation. Choose a natural symbol that resonates with your internal rhythms for the focus of this garden.

A meditation garden, while providing a focus, teaches us that what is apparent is only a minuscule part of the whole picture. What is hidden within us is uncovered through an inward journey.

PLACEMENT

Locate this garden in a place that ensures solitude, away from frequently traveled areas. Find a place that beckons and strips away tension and concern. This place may be blessed with the presence of a venerable oak tree or a bubbling stream, or it may be a patch of land just beyond a backyard knoll. When a place is found that makes your shoulders relax and your breathing slow down, the stage will be set for a meditative spirit to commence.

If your climate permits fewer than five months outside, consider creating an indoor meditation garden. Be sure that the room has a door and that you will not be disturbed. Consider an attic, a basement, or even a tub room as possible locations. I'm sure I am not the only person in the world to use a bathroom as a place for relaxing. A bathroom may be the only indoor space where it is acceptable to lock the door. The meditation area can consist of a bubble bath with vapors of steaming hot water or just a seat. Consider "time of use" as a factor in your choice. A main gathering room might be empty at 12 noon or 11 P.M. An office at 6 A.M. can also meet your needs. With a little creative thought you should be able to find a place where privacy is assured and time can be spent uninterrupted and free from distractions.

After you have chosen a location for your outdoor or indoor meditation garden, you should use it consistently to prepare your mind and body for tranquil contemplation. Consistency of use is desirable. I am not surprised to hear my stomach growling at approximately noon each day; likewise, I am comforted by sharing a kiss with my husband before I drift off to sleep. A good morning greeting to a colleague at work is a catalyst for feeling cheerful. Consistency reinforces intention. It is in our best interest to select a consistent time of day to use this garden.

Suggestions for Placement

A corner of an extra room
A side yard
A patch of land tucked behind a stand of trees
In the embrace of two perpendicular lines of a house or fence
A fenced-off side yard

Surrounded by nature and alone with our thoughts, we can dwell upon life's mysteries in a protected, cloistered garden. The value is as bottomless as our potential.

EDGES AND SHAPE

A meditation garden needs only one fairly thick edge to support and protect you. The edge, or wall, should be high enough to shield you from view. The vegetation on this wall should also be tall and full enough to hide the main feature of this garden. The other edges should be lower so you can be lured into this garden from other locations on your property.

Suggestions for the Edge

Living fence of pines
Bamboo
Cedar
Melaleuca
Eucalyptus
Fences made of wood, cement, stones, or brick

For a meditation area inside the home, a wall or a piece of furniture can be an edge. Even the back of a sofa can provide sufficient protection if you sit on the carpeted floor behind it as you meditate.

A figure eight is the favored shape for a meditation garden. The number eight is considered lucky, in part because it is the shape of infinity. Trace this figure with your finger and discover how the end leads back to the starting point; the beginnings and endings merge.

A tall border behind the seating area ensures privacy.

Understanding the significance of this shape can ultimately add to a sense of peace. With no beginning or end, our eyes tell us what our spirit knows—the source and the end are ultimately the same; it is the distance between that is important.

Pathways

The route to a meditation garden should be visible. Since there is no wrong moment to be drawn into this garden, the path should be clearly seen from both inside and outside a home. While the location should ensure privacy, the pathways leading to it should be visible and easy to walk on.

Upon crossing the threshold, be sure that the focus of the garden is partly seen, heard, or smelled. Don't let another feature obscure a direct view of the main feature.

Suggestions for Pathway Materials

Grass or gravel and stepping-stones
Decomposed granite and paving tiles
Bark chips or sand with stepping-stones

The Heart, or Focus, of the Garden

A boulder, a pond, a circle of abundance (a multitude of different plants creating the essence of wealth and contentment), a gazing ball, a sundial, cleared raked earth, or a strong aromatic fragrance can be the focus, or heart, of a meditation garden. The overall shape of the focal point should feel grounded, like a square earth shape. Don't get hung up on making it a perfect square. It is more important that the central feature communicates a sturdy, grounded presence.

Color is another important element of the center. Surround the heart with yellow or orange blooms. Yellow is a symbol of clarity of vision; orange is for communication. And most important, choose a central feature with a bearing that demands notice. The heart should command attention.

Suggestions for Objects as a Focal Point

Boulder
Pond

Raked earth
Circle of abundance
Scent

Suggestions for Vegetation as a Focal Point

Sequoia cactus
Dwarf apple
Dwarf pine
Gold-dust tree

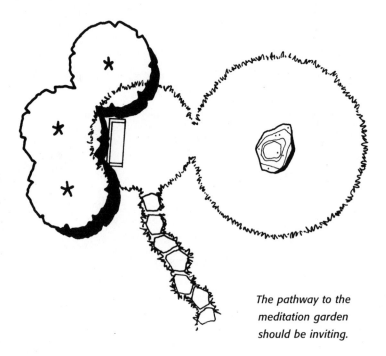

*The pathway to the
meditation garden
should be inviting.*

If you select a circle of abundance as the focal point, be sure
to fill it with plants that will not become snack food for animals.
Nothing could be more ironic than having abundance nibbled away.
Choose animal-resistant plants. Moreover, be careful to avoid plants
that naturalize and spread at the expense of others, such as yarrow
or Mexican evening primrose. The plant that represents abundance
in one season could become tomorrow's weed. (See Chapter 8.)

Deer-Resistant Plantings for the Circle of Abundance

A variety of factors contributes to the deer-resistant qualities of plants. Poisonous flowers or leaves, unpleasant textures (they find fuzzy foliage distasteful), and aromatic plants are all deterrents. Note, however, we can't guarantee the following plants as deer-proof. Tastes sometimes change. Plants that deer ignore one year may be irresistible to them the next.

The following list represents a sampling of plant material that deer do not seem to find terribly appealing. Be sure to consult the master plant list in the back of the book for more options.

Trees

Fir (*Abies*)
Acacia (*Acacia*)
Mimosa (*Albizia*)
Smoke tree (*Cotinus*)
Spruce (*Picea*)

Shrubs

Butterfly bush (*Buddleia*)
Wild lilac (*Ceanothus*)
Rockrose (*Cistus*)
Cotoneaster (*Cotoneaster*)

Vines and Ground Covers

Manzanita (*Arctostaphylos*)
Clematis (*Clematis*)
Jasmine (*Jasminum*)
Blue star creeper (*Laurentia*)
Cape honeysuckle (*Tecomaria*)

Perennials

Windflower (*Anemone*)
Wormwood (*Artemisia*)
Bleeding heart (*Dicentra*)
Foxglove (*Digitalis*)
Blanketflower (*Gaillardia* × *grandiflora*)

PLANTS AND OTHER FEATURES

Where is it written that a garden must have many varieties of vegetation? According to Webster's dictionary, a garden is a delightful spot, and ironically, we often delight in the absence of detail. Feng shui teaches us to consider what motivates us to change. Simplicity of design, detail, and color may be the perfect choice for an area of contemplation.

While one edge of this garden can be backed by a stand of vegetation that is skirted to the ground and the focal point can be filled with a flowering circle of abundance, a meditation garden may have very few other growing features. Stones, sand, or low-growing ground cover can provide the foil against which the main feature is viewed. The gently curved lines of the garden's shape should be filled with a still presence to carry the eye to the focal point.

When completed, a meditation garden should help you experience the profundity of nonmovement. It should be still, but not quiet, infused with the sort of peacefulness that elicits deep change. Strength can be derived by associating with the immutable. A meditation garden should lead inside.

12

A Lover's Garden

Compassion

Consecration

Liberation

Devotion

W hether it's the love of life, another person, or an idea, a lover's garden affirms nuances of devotion. Remember when you first met a mate or a friend, saw your newborn, or read a book that changed your life? What at first was dazzling grew deep and lasting. Love's flourishes are small compared with its strong, thick roots. And so it is with a lover's garden. After the drama of beginnings, as you venture deeper into the experience, the fullness of love is revealed. The entrance to a lover's garden is breathtaking, but it only hints at what is inside.

A garden for lovers is heavy with fragrances and layered with a mélange of colors, and at its core is a setting of privacy. Privacy gives us permission to be comfortable and reveal our inner core. Love allows us to bare our soul without concern for ridicule or recrimination. With the full acceptance that love affords, we can dare to be who we genuinely are.

Love and the expression of love inspire the use of symbols, as poets throughout the ages have demonstrated. Plants also convey symbolic meanings and should be chosen carefully for inclusion in the lover's garden. Consult the section in Chapter 7 on plants and their meanings, and choose plants and features that express your innermost feelings about love. For example, if the core of your love is acceptance, a pool of water at the center of the garden can be perfect to represent the depth of your receptivity. A rare bloom such as an orchid, purple dahlia, or flowering cactus can reveal the care you are willing to bring to a relationship, an ideal, or a job. However we choose to express it, the meaning of plants can affect the process and expression of love.

Creating a garden to honor love is a testament to life's highest purpose. A lover's garden is the mirror we hold up to reflect what we give and to suggest what we anticipate receiving.

Imagine this. Just beyond a path's curve or a door's swing, a gateway springs from the earth. It is an enticing threshold that attracts you. You are compelled to grasp your loved one's hand and duck underneath this first arbor, in the same way as square dancers crouch underneath the upraised hands of other dancers as they wend their way around a circle. Emerging from the first threshold, you are surrounded by slender stalks that roll in the breeze and strain to greet you. The air is filled with fragrances as you follow a path until reaching the second threshold, which is thicker, lower, and more mysterious. Inside the second chamber is a square clearing edged with thick, full vegetation that guarantees privacy. In the center is another garden called the circle of two. Whether the circle of two is large enough to lie down in or whether it is so small that it contains two single plants is less important than the fact that you see a place from which you can perch and contemplate the circle of two. Be it a bench, a velvety blanket of grass, or a boulder, there is a place to reflect inside this inner sanctum—a place to spend time with thoughts of the appreciation of love. Thus, this space calls you to its embrace, and your love is reinforced by the magic of nature.

> *"Love is not primarily a relationship to a specific person; it is an attitude, an orientation of character which determines the relatedness of a person to the world as a whole, not towards one 'object' of love. . . . If I truly love one person I love all persons, I love the world, I love life. . . . I love through you the world, I love in you also myself."*
>
> Erich Fromm

PLACEMENT

Whereas the entrance to the lover's garden is obvious, what lies beyond it is not. A gate, the arching branches of a birch tree, morning glories climbing a string suspended between two trees, or a trellis with an opening incised in the center can be the frames supporting the first threshold. The path leading from it enchants as it wends its way to another threshold entrance.

Suggestions for Placement of the First Threshold

Just outside a side or back door
At the edge of a woods
An arbor over a stairway leading outside

The first threshold should be wide enough for two persons to walk through hand-in-hand. This entrance must be both lush and strong.

The first threshold

**Suggestions for Aromatic Climbing Plants
on the First Threshold**

Jasmine varieties
Honeysuckle
Vine lilac
Climbing rose

The plantings surrounding this first entrance should inundate us with their fragrance.

EDGES AND SHAPE

The Passageway

A lover's garden has two rooms. The first room is merely a large walkway leading to the inner sanctum. From this path we can only glimpse a fraction of what lies ahead. Mystery fuels the desire to proceed. I used an existing passageway along the side of our home as the first chamber. It continues to the end of the house and then the pathway leads around a corner to an arched bough that frames the inner chamber. All I had to add to this first area were the edging plants.

Adorn the first pathway with plants from mid-calf to hip high to allow breezes to caress the body while permitting the sight of a distant vista. Only when passing through the second threshold will the edging material be higher and more prominent, blocking what is beyond.

The pathway material might be a fine grass, sand, or pine needles. Sprinkle low-growing, fragrant pink, deep purple, or raspberry blossoms on the edge of the path. The aromatic delights of the blossoms fill the air and energize the visitor to traverse the route to the inner chamber.

Suggestions for Edging Plants in the First Area

Fern varieties
Azalea varieties
Gardenia
Evergreen grasses
Rhododendron

The Inner Sanctum

The second room, an inner sanctum, does not lie straight ahead but sits off to one side. This protected position fosters feelings of safety and security, the way love ought to do. For the same reason, this chamber is a square earth shape, which also instills groundedness.

To guard against prying eyes, thick, full edges should surround the inner sanctum. Trees whose branches sweep toward the earth, stalks that are covered with leaves, or bushes with branches that wave like the arms of the Hindu god Siva are recommended. Because the edges obscure our view to the outside, we are compelled to focus inward after we have entered the stable, square shape of the chamber.

Suggestions for Edging Plants in the Inner Sanctum

Pittosporum varieties
Rhododendron
Raphiolepis varieties

Suggestions for Edging Trees in the Inner Sanctum

Willow myrtle
California pepper tree

Mayten
Weeping willow

Since the varieties within a species can vary dramatically, be sure to check with a local expert to confirm the mature heights of all plant materials. Both love and plants need room to blossom but not grow out of control.

Guarding the portal of the inner sanctum, like sentinels, can be two trees or bushes, one representing the male and the other, the female. These plants underscore the need for balance. Fruit trees are likely choices because many have both male and female varieties. If you cannot find male and female plants of the same variety, choose vegetation that expresses the virtues of both yin (female) and yang (male). For example, one can have dark leaves or bark (yin); the other, light leaves and bark (yang).

Suggestions for Male and Female Plantings

Alder
Carob
Fruit trees

The Heart, or Focus, of the Garden Inside the Inner Sanctum

A Circle of Two

A circle connotes equality and is a symbol of commitment. Our eyes tend to stay within the confines of a circle's circumference, and we are not inclined to mentally wander. A wedding band, which would truly fit a finger better if its shape were elliptical, is fashioned into a circle, perhaps because a circle's underlying meaning underscores the connection and commitment necessary for lovers.

Either a large circle, one that practically takes up all the space, or a circle large enough for two plants is in the center of the inner sanctum. If a large circle is selected, fill it with pairs of flowers or place two of a species on the border of the circle, leaving an opening spacious enough for a couple to lie down. Whatever the love object is, relationships begin with two. Whether it is you and another person, an idea, or a wish, two is the starting point for love. At the edge of the circle of two, plant flowers that produce orange blooms or trees that have an orangish bark. Orange affirms the rich possibilities of fusion.

Since the essence of love suggests giving more than receiving, plants that require our devotion and special attention are desirable. The circle of two is not maintenance-free in the same way that a love object is never free from our caring, attention, and focus. This would be a good place to consider using annuals, such as marigolds, because they require fairly frequent replacement and attention to look their best.

If your climate or your preference prevents you from sitting on the ground, provide comfortable seating that faces the entrance and the circle of two. Feng shui dictates that we need to see the entrance to a room if we want to completely relax or concentrate. Therefore, the position that nurtures and protects when lying in bed, working at a desk, or sitting in the inner sanctum of a lover's garden is the position facing an entrance or door.

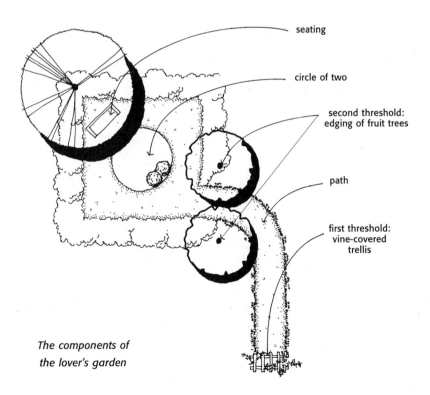

seating

circle of two

second threshold: edging of fruit trees

path

first threshold: vine-covered trellis

The components of the lover's garden

Make sure the seating area facing the circle of two is large enough to accommodate more than one person comfortably. When choosing the seat, consider using a tree log, a plank supported by two stones, or a wrought-iron bench.

Suggestions for Edging Plants in the Circle of Two

Sweet woodruff
Chamomile

PATHWAYS

How the road is traveled is just as important as reaching the final destination. The path to and within a lover's garden must be effortless to walk upon. Stepping-stones that require you to watch your footing are not a good pathway choice for this garden. The earth must be level and free of roots and rocks. If you feel you could travel on this path in darkness and still feel secure, then you have provided the perfect route for a lover's garden.

This garden is meant to be shared; therefore, one pathway, wide enough for two people to walk side by side, is best. A path that requires one person to lead and the other to follow only reinforces the notion of inequality. In the best of all situations, love is reciprocated, and all involved are equal.

Suggestions for Pathway Materials

Grass
Sand
Raked earth
Smooth stone gravel

Love is a synergistic consciousness. Herbert L. Leff in his book, *Playful Perceptions*, writes "Synergy refers to combined action, where contributions reinforce each other." With conscious awareness of how we affect others, an effort to creatively synthesize our innate nature with another's need, desire, and intention is at the core of the process called loving.

13

HEALING GARDEN

Restoration

Replenishment

Relinquishment

Renewal

Many of us were born in perfect emotional and physical health; however, life's circumstances, as well as our genetic predisposition, alter this healthy state. How we care for ourselves and how we perceive our state of health, in large part, determine the quality of our well-being. To be healed is to obliterate all interference and reclaim our wholeness and wellness. A healing garden reestablishes an alliance with optimal physical, emotional, and spiritual health and allows us to tap into the best and highest sources both universally and humanly available. Why do we feel we have to do it alone when we have at our beck and call the entire universe as an ally?

Healing restores a feeling of unimpeachable wholeness and contentment. A healing garden supports a belief that there is a way to eject our despair or dysfunction. The first step in healing is to replace despondence with hope. Who among us has not pondered the vastness of the universe while gazing at the night sky? The sky represents mystery and the promise of what was, what is, and what will be. We experience its physical form as eternity. The objective of a healing garden lies in the knowledge that there is a road to renewal.

Thus, a healing garden feels familiar in a positive way and assists in establishing the knowledge that we can heal our body, mind, and spirit. A healing garden helps us know that, within the confines of the moment, there is access to freedom from pain, sorrow, and fear. We need a combination of hope, clarity, and resolve to begin our healing, and conviction is the first step on our journey.

PLACEMENT

What is your favorite outdoor space? Is it under a huge maple tree in the backyard or in a nook in the side yard? Is it associated with a positive past experience? Walk around your property and find an area that feels right. If you notice an area where your head feels clearer or your shoulders less tense, you have found the right spot for your healing garden.

If your healing garden must be indoors, choose a private place that you can rearrange and be sequestered in.

Suggestions for Placement

Nestled in an L-shaped corner
In a gazebo

Near a windowless outside wall
Under a willow or other tree with branches that droop to the
   ground
A section of a covered porch
Under an outdoor umbrella

Shape and Edges

The shape of the garden is less important than the amount of space.
A healing garden should be small enough to feel womblike. If you
were to stretch out your arms, the walls would be within reach.
Although our connections to family and friends are critical to the
healing process, our mind, body, and spirit ultimately restructure
our health. This garden has just enough space for us to feel comfortable, but not so much that it makes us feel powerless.

Above all, a healing garden should make you feel safe. If you
are self-conscious about being seen, position this garden away from
any nearby buildings, windows, or doors. The number of walls
around your garden will depend upon personal requirements for
privacy.

To create a private garden, place a trellis against a wall, plant
bushes around a tree, or grow tall willows near a pond. Tall plants
or vines can be trained upward to create a perimeter for this garden. Blooms that cascade from trellised vines overhead will direct
energy back to earth and help you remain connected.

A ceiling is an unusual feature to devise outdoors, but it is
indispensable to a healing garden. Light shining through a distinct
opening in the ceiling is an essential ingredient in a healing garden.
Well-being begins with hope, and sunlight produces optimism.
Whether we feel the light on our body or view it contemplatively,
a ceiling with a skylight can permeate the space with hopefulness.

Here are some suggestions that may help you locate, construct,
or embellish an outdoor ceiling.

Suggestions for Creating an Outdoor Ceiling

A tree with branches that span at least 36 inches from the
   trunk
A fast-growing, leafy plant with a slender stalk that can be
   trained to drape overhead. Like the gardeners who train the
   thick-stemmed bonsai trees, you can coax plants to bend to
   shape a ceiling.

Garden wire fastened between two trellises to support ceiling
 growth
Ties and bolts mounted on an outside wall or fence to guide
 vines across an area
For drier climates where leafy vegetation is hard
 to maintain, use a wood trellis, canvas,
 or rip-stop sailing material
 in lieu of plants.
Tie branches to form a tepee,
 leaving an opening at the
 apex for light.

**Suggestions for
Ceiling Plants**

Clematis
Jasmine
Wisteria

*A nook in the side
yard with trained
vines for the ceiling*

PATHWAYS

A healing garden is a private space; it is not typically shared. While
there does not need to be a defined path, the entrance needs a distinctive adornment. Since our eyes are automatically attracted to
refracted light and moving objects, a mobile of stars or a crystal that
captures light can be the siren that lures you inside.

Suggestions for Objects at the Entrance

Crystal
Mobile
Wind chime
Gazing ball
Decorative object with reflective surfaces

The Heart, or Focus, of the Garden

You are the heart of a healing garden. What you choose to sit on—a lounge chair, blanket, stool, bench, or rock—is less important than your comfort. Place a seat underneath the opening in the ceiling. This opening to the sky is a metaphor for the light at the end of the tunnel or a ray of hope, or it can be regarded as the path toward healing.

Suggestions for Seating

Wood-slat lounge chair
Metal chair with a cushion that can be scrubbed clean
Plastic lounge chair

Plants and Other Features

Low-growing plants with small blooms are best in the healing garden because the interior space typically will be small. Use ferns, mosses, and other plants that have texture or delicate designs and don't require a great deal of sunlight.

If it's more convenient or if the soil won't support growth, choose plants that are pleasant to caress and plant them in terra cotta containers close to the seating.

The rest of the garden floor should be soft and inviting. Cover a rocky surface with pine needles, comb the grass to remove stones or debris, or sift the sand to get rid of sharp pieces of shells. In part, healing involves filtering from within. By filtering out harmful or unpleasant objects from this garden's foundation you outwardly duplicate the healing process.

Suggestions for Ground Cover

Baby's tears
Blue star creeper
Shredded bark
Sand

A healing garden is designed to provide a comfortable place to rest, a pleasant texture to stroke, and light streaming in from above to evoke hope. Our body truly strives for balance that embraces mental, physical, and spiritual health. Creating a place away from the swirl of everyday living grants admission to this process.

14

A Child's Garden

Unself-consciousness

Adventurousness

Freedom

Joy

Childhood is a state of mind. Although this chapter is written as if childhood were a period on a chronological time line, a child's garden is for anyone who dares to abandon constraints, to fill an afternoon with laughter, to be curious about simple things, and to be unhindered by worry about appearances. By saturating a space with experiences, this garden nurtures curiosity. Curiosity is the single most important human trait that separates a life of boredom from a life of wonder. Exploring without the fear of being harmed or doing wrong teaches us to be brave.

When I was a child, I lived next to a forest. Under an ever-changing canopy of leaves, I whiled away hours examining pine cones, stumps, and rivulets of water dribbling down a sloping terrain. Children love to scrutinize all kinds of minutiae, and a garden that encourages investigation will provide memories for a lifetime.

Children need space to exercise large motor skills. In an outdoor area, jumping, rolling, and running are not likely to be interrupted by bumping into or breaking objects. Having room to move about freely is essential in a child's garden.

Children like to climb. My friend Barnaby romps all over the back of his family's sofa as he bellows his ideas for all to hear. Perched higher than the people around him, Barnaby uses his climbing skills to bolster his importance. The truth is that Barnaby would be heard, even if he proffered his thoughts while hiding under the dining room table, but climbing gives him a vantage point that, at five years old, he doesn't naturally have.

Part of the fun of climbing is the exhilaration of falling. The joy of landing comfortably on a pile of autumn leaves, a carpet of thick grass, or a mound of freshly fallen snow is the carefree quality that often wanes as we age. If possible, a child's garden should contain objects to climb and soft places to fall.

This garden should also include hiding places. Some games change over the decades, but the game of hide-and-seek has survived. The excitement of hiding is outmatched only by the thrill of finding. A game of hide-and-seek teaches the young to take action based upon observation. A thick tree trunk; a bush with long, weeping branches; a tree house; or a staggered fence are places that children can use to camouflage their whereabouts.

A water feature is another desirable element. Water is a magnet. A pond in front of my home, which is no bigger than an arm's length in either direction, is visited daily by the neighborhood children. Peering into the water to look for tadpoles, splashing their hands, or just staring at the trickle of water that flows down a volcanic rock perched at one side delights them endlessly. Since safety is always a consideration, I have surrounded the pond with stones taller than waist high to make it highly unlikely that a child could fall in. Water in some safe form is essential for this garden.

When implementing plans for the child's garden, it is important to include children in as many activities as possible. The first time I saw a tomato plant, I was seven years old. What a marvel it was to see the hefty, succulent red sphere hanging from the slender green stalk! Children are amazed to learn the process of how vegetables develop before they arrive at the supermarket.

When my son Zachary was a child, I sectioned off a small plot of land within my perennial garden. He could choose and plant whatever he wanted there. Some years it would be a disaster, such as when the mint he chose devoured the flowers. Other years we could harvest garlic and onions from his fertile patch. The year he left for college, this tiny patch had garlic, yarrow, and pansies. To this day, when he returns home, he looks at his garden to discover what I've done with it.

Gardening teaches important lessons. Fulfilling a responsibility over a long time is frequently rewarded with success, but sometimes it is not. Learning that joy comes more from the process than the results is a model for life. Tending a plant teaches us this lesson.

Thus, a child's garden is a mélange of delights, with just enough structure to suggest order, but not too much fabrication to limit adventure. A tire hung from a tree, a small hollow in the earth, a log placed in the ideal spot, and a cleared strip of earth for planting are just some of the simple delights that you can include in an outdoor child's room.

PLACEMENT

Children are not naturally cautious. They leap before they look and grab before they analyze. It is normal to expect them to experience some bumps and bruises at play. Therefore, when planning a child's garden, locate it within earshot or where it can be seen easily. Sometimes adult intervention is necessary.

Suggestions for Placement

In view of a room typically used by an adult during the hours
   children are outside
On a front lawn, as long as there is a barrier to the road
In a backyard
In a playroom adjoining an adult's area

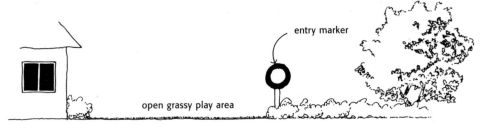

entry marker

open grassy play area

Children should be seen and heard as they play.

SHAPE AND EDGES

The contour of this garden will be ordained by existing vegetation. The shape will be determined by features such as trees, high bushes, boulders, open spaces, hiding places, inclines and flatlands, high boughs, and caves. As you plan a child's garden, allow for both open spaces (yang) and small spaces (yin) to represent balance.

A low edge allows an adult observer to maintain safety. Permitting opportunities for physical exuberance and parental watchfulness are a benefit of keeping the border low.

Low-Growing Plants for the Border

Lilyturf
Lavender
Rockrose

PATHWAYS

An open expanse of land can lead to a child's garden because traditional paths are much too constrained for the exuberance of children. The entrance, however, should be defined by a sense of fun and magic. Children love fantasy and whimsy and will delight in having an enchanting gateway to an outdoor world. Don't be daunted by these suggestions. You will be surprised at how easily something can be constructed or arranged.

Suggestions for an Enchanting Entrance

1. Mount two posts in the ground with a 12-inch flat wooden board on top. Epoxy a plastic globe on top of the board, and paint it a bright color. Give this entrance an enchanting name, such as "The Lollipop Palace."
2. Purchase stuffed animals from a local thrift shop and tack them to a post. No, they won't last forever, but neither will childhood.
3. Mount old tires on a pole. They can also be used as targets through which balls can be thrown.

Cast convention to the wind. Invent ideas and construct an entrance to a child's garden that stops the eye and tickles the imagination. My son will never forget the day we cleared an area in the woods around a motorless rusted-out Mercedes left by the property's former owners. We named it "Greased Lightning," and we spray-painted it all sorts of colors and drew a big happy face on the trunk. After removing the vehicle's back doors, the back seat became an "Alice in Wonderland" tunnel entrance to a woodland garden.

THE HEART, OR FOCUS, OF THE GARDEN

A child's garden needs options. Instead of thinking of this garden as a room, think of it as an entire house. Areas for running, climbing, water fun, planting, hiding, and sitting are some of the rooms that can constitute the whole. However, feng shui guidelines suggest that a home without a heart is empty of soul, and all those living inside will scatter like birds scared from a resting perch. A moving object is a wonderful heart in a child's garden because things that respond to movement are likely to inspire concentration. For that reason, traditional feng shui practitioners install wind chimes as a cure for many ills. A usable play object, such as a swing, is a natural for the heart of a child's garden.

> *How do you like to go up in a swing,*
> *Up in the air so blue?*
> *Oh, I do think it the pleasantest thing*
> *Ever a child can do!*
> Robert Louis Stevenson,
> A Child's Garden of Verses

Swinging engages all the senses. The eyes see new vistas, the skin feels the air differently, the nose inhales more deeply, and the ears fill with the sounds of pumping the swing. All these senses are stimulated in the seconds it takes to careen up in the air and down.

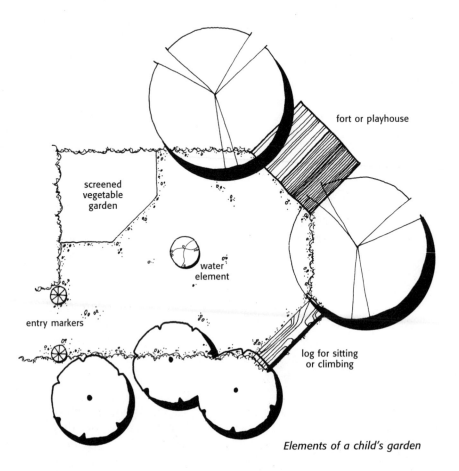

Elements of a child's garden

Suggestions for the Heart

A tire hanging from a knotted rope

A plank of wood suspended from a tree bough by two strong
straps

Colorful, lightweight nylon ribbons hanging from a pole
or tree

A helicopter rescue net dancing from a basketball pole

A barrel held aloft by ropes

An assortment of lightweight birdhouses, hanging at varying
heights from tree branches

OTHER CONSIDERATIONS IN A CHILD'S GARDEN

Running

Children fly to the things they love. If possible, there should be
enough distance between the house and the garden to allow children to dash around.

Climbing

Lean a log in the crevice of a stump or construct a stand on which
it can rest. Keep the ground underneath and around a climbing
object free from stones or roots that could scratch or puncture a
child's skin.

Water Feature

If there are no natural water features, make one. (Most local building departments have code regulations that govern the installation
of a pond, pool, or any other container. Check the regulations
before installing a water feature.) Here's a simple suggestion. Install
an adapter on an outdoor water spigot, and attach a garden hose
to it. Mount a sprinkler valve on the other end, and thread it
through a hole in a plastic pail. Voilà! You have an instant mini foun-
tain! Be sure to allow the water to drain off by digging a drain or
ditch or placing this feature on a high part of the land.

Planting

Let the children select the plants for the plot of land designated as
the vegetable garden or flower bed. If they are like my son, they
will want a huge garden. But just as setting limits for behavior is

beneficial, limiting the size of the garden will afford more opportunity for success, mainly because it will be manageable.

Select hardy, easy-to-care-for plants that are likely to survive some extremes, such as overzealous watering and an occasional trodding on when a ball gets away from the catcher. Grow flowers with large, colorful blooms and vegetables that are normally eaten by the family. Nothing is more thrilling for a child than to stand on a chair with a parent close by and to cut his or her first tomato or to tear apart a homegrown pumpkin and scoop out the pulpy pie material. My own son's eyes sparkled with enthusiasm as I cheered him on by announcing, like a circus ringmaster, "Ladies and gentlemen, I present you Mr. Zachary, chef extraordinaire!"

Suggestions for Vegetation in a Planting Area

Things to Grow

Wild strawberries
Blackberries
Tomatoes
Corn
Carrots
Peas
Ornamental kale
Pumpkins
Sunflowers

Things to Pick

Pansies
Daisies
Violets
Violas
Bellflowers
Nigellas
Snapdragons
Primroses
Nasturtiums

Things to Smell

Mint
Geraniums
Gardenias

Lilacs
Jasmine
Lavender
Breath of heaven
Rosemary

Things to Astonish

Red-hot pokers for wands
Strawflowers
Gourds for containers
Willows to cut for magic wands
Bamboo for spyglasses or for making trumpet sounds
Aloe to rub on cuts
Plants that attract birds and butterflies

Hiding

Whether in a large enclosure with enough room for several people or in a tiny space into which one small body can barely squeeze, hiding is fun! Caves, tree houses, and tepees can be a child's first personal dwelling. If your yard is bereft of a natural enclosure, consider making one. Long, thin grasses or plants that can be parted like a theater curtain and flutter in the wind are natural hiding places.

Suggestions for Making Hiding Places

Canvas draped over a pole
Tablecloth tossed over a heavy cardboard box
Branches or palm fronds piled high
Cornstalks
Pole beams
Tall grasses

Sitting

Who doesn't remember having an important childhood meeting outdoors? Whether it was to share the rules of a game or a funny story or to chat about nothing in particular, a place to sit is a must in the child's garden.

Children don't necessarily need chairs because they rarely sit still. While conversing, they may use the tip of a slender twig to inscribe lines in the dusty earth, swing their legs, or generally fidget and squirm around.

Suggestions for Seating

Tree stump
Mound of earth
Log
Boulders
Soft grass
Pine needles
Fallen branches

To be intimate and feel at home outside, to use our body in ways we typically do not, to experience our surroundings differently, to revel in the wonders of what is and what can be, to be joyous and free—all are the underpinnings of a child's garden, which will delight, entertain, and teach.

15

FERTILITY GARDEN

Production

Patience

Prolificity

Fruitfulness

A fertility garden should abound with life. Since life begets life, having overflowing, healthy plant life is a metaphor for our own abundance. Whether our desire is to be fertile with life, love, friends, or other rewards, having a fertility garden will manifest our desire. Although most of us respond emotionally to a place, the true experience of a place is located in our brain stem, not in our midbrain (the emotions) nor in the neocortex (the intellect). In the same way that our lungs take in air and our heart pumps blood, our response to a place is automatic and involuntary.

It takes energy to be fertile. Stimulation awakens energy. The stimulation of colors, motion, and forms can energize an outdoor scape. Wind chimes, mobiles, or hummingbird feeders bring in movement, sound, and color and are excellent items for animating a garden.

In contrast to stimulation, patience, a quality not often associated with fertility, is a hidden factor in garnering abundance. Our American view of time often precludes feeling relaxed about reaching a goal, especially when achieving the goal takes more "time" than we originally wanted. However, the more agitated we become, the less likely it becomes that we will achieve our goal. Patience and inner peacefulness give us the serenity to act and do our best.

In his book, *The Dance of Life,* Edward T. Hall describes how Westerners view time as fixed and feel compelled to accomplish things within an artificial, self-imposed framework. He suggests that we think of time as a commodity that can stand still and be wasted or used, and once it passes, it can be forever lost. This, however, is not how all cultures view time. In the Hopi culture, "the experience of time . . . is more natural—like breathing, a rhythmic part of life." To the Hopis, then, the quality of patience doesn't battle the clock.

A fertility garden helps us relax. Tension, caused by stress, contributes to many modern-day ills. We are on the alert more often than we care to admit. How can we possibly be effective when we are not serene? A fertility garden, while stimulating our soul, helps diminish our physical and mental tensions.

To be fertile is to be prolific. For me, this conjures up words spilling out of my mind onto a writing surface. For another person, being prolific could mean juggling a career, an exercise program, and a family. To some, a bountiful life would include having opportunities to meet a mate or to become pregnant. Whatever being prolific or fertile means to us personally, we all have areas in our life that we wish would explode, enlarge, expand, or extend, and fertility ultimately means personal enrichment.

The wisdom of feng shui dictates that when we need to expand upon ideas, careers, or family, we would be best served by a profusion of symbols in our visual field. Seeing two tulips, two peony bushes, or two roses in a tall-stemmed vase fuels our capability to grow and reproduce.

PLACEMENT

A fertility garden can be placed either outdoors or indoors. It can be permanent and rooted in soil or as temporary as fresh-cut flowers in a vase of water. For those who want to surround their intention with ritual or for those whose wish list changes often, a fresh-flower fertility garden is the most suitable.

Becoming fertile is often a temporary process, depending on the specific results we desire. Therefore, we may, over the course of a year, have several fertility gardens for completely different reasons. For example, if you wish to become pregnant, a bedroom might be the appropriate place for a fertility garden. If you have writer's block, place a fertility garden next to your computer. Regardless of where you place a fertility garden, the more this garden is in view, the greater its impact will be.

Suggestions for Placement

What You Desire	Where to Place the Garden	Soil or Water
Abundance of business	In view of a desk or work area	Soil
Pregnancy	Bedroom	Soil or water
A relationship	In the far right-hand corner of a gathering room	Soil
Mental growth	To the left of an entrance to a workroom, library, or gathering space	Soil
A satisfying career	In the center of the back wall of a main gathering space	Soil
Good test grades	On the left side of a desk or study table	Water

By keeping this garden close at hand, you will be more likely to absorb its influence.

SHAPE AND EDGES

Select a container that speaks to your soul, a vessel that delights you aesthetically or evokes fond memories. A rectangular or oblong shape is preferred for this container because this shape implies growth and change. Even if you decide to create this garden outdoors, the vessel is as important as the plants.

Obscure the edge with plants, because fertility implies an absence of boundaries. A profusion of plants that spill over the edges creates a visual metaphor for the concept of flourishing.

Suggestions for Indoor Plants for the Edges

Ivy varieties
Philodendron

PATHWAYS

The path to a fertility garden is a pathway for the eyes, instead of the body. Position the fertility garden's container in a room that corresponds to the intention. Be sure nothing obscures your view of the garden; move any accessories or furniture to the side. To command your visual attention, be sure a lamp's cone of light is fully directed on the container.

THE HEART, OR FOCUS, OF THE GARDEN

Consider how water triumphs through its perseverance to erode rock or even carve canyons out of mountains. Like water, you must let nothing get in the way. We all have heard stories about how famous authors were rejected again and again before their books were accepted. If James Redfield had been daunted by rejection, *The Celestine Prophecy* would not have been published. A large publishing house accepted it only after his self-published book had become a hit. If failure had disheartened and discouraged him from taking other actions, success would have never been his. Perseverance often separates the people who achieve success from those who are stymied by initial defeat.

Use water or a symbol for water, such as a black stone or a

curved object, at the heart of your fertility garden, and place it where it can't be seen. Determination is at the heart of all positive actions, but it is apparent only to the person who is involved in the process. Placing a hidden water symbol in the center of a fertility garden is a way of internalizing determination.

Suggestions for the Heart

Black stone
Small container
Dream catcher
Bowl of water
Geode with a wavy pattern

Naturally, fresh flowers in a vase will not need a water symbol. For those who need resolve and determination up front, a glass container will not let them forget that persistence is always a necessary ingredient of fertility.

PLANTS AND OTHER FEATURES

A profusion of vegetation should occupy the rest of the space in the fertility garden. Let the choice of plants or flowers correspond to your desires and the seasons. Consider the meanings of plants (Chapter 7), and select ones that resonate with your wishes.

Suggestions for Plants in Soil

African violet
Kaffir lily
Orchid

Suggestions for Plants in Water

Gladiolus
Gerbera
Lily
Rose

A fertility garden engenders hopefulness and can symbolize optimism in the face of the unknown. It is, perhaps, the most versatile, yet most fleeting, of all the gardens. Therefore we must replace, restore, and regenerate our resolve to encase experiences with an awareness of originality. The fertility garden reminds us to ferret out the best of ourselves and not be fearful.

16

WINTER'S GARDEN

Encouragement

Energy

Light

Amusement

If you feel gloomy during the coldest months of the year, then a winter's garden can be the perfect antidote. Studies conducted to ascertain why native Alaskans don't suffer as much from depression as people from the lower forty-eight states have determined that Alaskans tolerate the darkness and biting cold by spending as much time as possible outside. Going outdoors is clearly a way to counterbalance the cabin fever that afflicts many people who live in cold climates with shortened daylight hours.

The reduced quantity of sunlight adds to winter's forbidding quality. Many of us arise in darkness and return home at nightfall. Scientists have discovered a hormone triggered by sunlight that adds to a sense of optimism. For some of us, the lack of sufficient sunlight or full-spectrum lighting can cause seasonal affective disorder (SAD). Adding full-spectrum light to a winter's scene can counteract the blahs.

Many view the outdoors as an enemy in colder weather, but the true enemies are the toxins from building materials and other products that escape into our airtight homes. Volatile organic compounds (VOCs) from formaldehyde and other substances added to glues, composite woods, and other synthetic materials are literally exhaled into the air. We seal in these poisons by building airtight homes. Going outside gives us the opportunity to replenish ourselves with cleaner air. Naturally, if you can't go outside, fill your indoor spaces with plants that consume toxins (see Chapter 8).

Another problem with winter is the lack of vibrant color. Bare branches and white snow often combine to create a severe, colorless landscape. Color, as discussed in Chapter 5, is more than a visual treat. Inherent in every color is a message that stimulates, soothes, or reinforces an emotional or physical state. Without a choice of color, we expend additional energy on the resources we need to sustain contentment. A winter's garden restores color and meaning to the landscape.

Although it is not typical in the sense of planting, caring, and reaping, a winter's garden can help counteract cabin fever, gray skies, and the restriction of mobility that cold weather often imposes. This garden, like all gardens, is seasonal. A winter's garden will force you to go outside to have a good time because the heart of this garden changes and requires attention. This garden can restore and refresh us with renewed chi (energy) during a normally dormant time of year.

PLACEMENT

A winter's garden should not be seen from a window in a room in which you spend a great deal of time. We sometimes stop noticing a scene when it becomes too familiar. Therefore, locate the garden outside a window near a stair landing or a back door or at the end of a hallway to ensure that this garden will remain novel and entertaining.

Suggestions for Placement

Outside a stairway window
Near a door with a glass pane
Outside a bathroom window
Near a hallway window

SHAPE AND EDGES

The size, shape, and edges of a winter's garden will be determined by the way it is viewed. If it is observed from a picture window, the garden needs to be wide enough to make a strong statement. If a winter's garden is seen between the mullions of a back door, it could be narrow. The edges of a winter's garden need to fill the frame of the window from which the garden is viewed. The entire edge should surround the scene, much like a picture frame around a painting.

Like the perspective in a landscape painting, the pathway edges will lead the eye to the focal point. If the plants are dormant, use stones or logs or build a snow wall topped with rocks or sticks to define the edges.

Suggestions for Edging Plants

Juniper varieties
Cotoneaster
Currant
Gooseberry

Barberry
Yew
Arborvitae
Russian olive

Suggestions for Edging Materials

Rocks
Solar lights in snowbanks
Logs
Snow sculpture

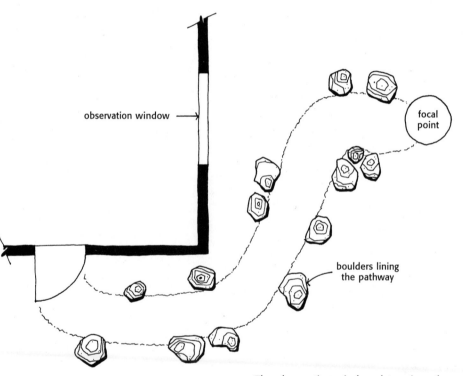

The observation window determines the size, shape, and edging of the garden.

PATHWAYS

The pathway to this garden should start at a frequently used entrance because you will be visiting the heart of this garden often to rearrange a stone, add seeds to a bird feeder, or stick a fresh carrot on a snowman's face. Since this garden is meant to lure you outside, the pathway leading to it needs to be convenient, as well as enticing.

Whether you use solar or low-voltage lights or even painted rocks, add color and light along the pathway to the winter's garden.

The Heart, or Focus, of the Garden

Choosing the focus, or heart, of a winter's garden is the best part because it can be as simple or as elaborate as you wish. When my son was young, we would adjust the central elements after every snowfall or whenever one of the elements in our garden melted. Yes, we had snow people as the focus of most of our winter gardens. Sometimes we made snow families. Sometimes the head of the snowman was topped with a Frisbee/bird feeder. And always the faces were garnished with a variety of foodstuffs, from carrot eyes to cauliflower hair. The objective of the central focus is to infuse something lighthearted into a bleak time of year.

It is also appropriate to use more stately features in the heart. A "formal" focal point could be an evergreen tree, gazing ball, gate, bird feeder, or wood pile. Select an object that does not visibly change in cold weather and that provides a splash of color. A red-twig dogwood or a red hummingbird feeder stands out against a stark landscape. Whatever you use as the focus of a winter's garden, the object itself is less important than its presence, color, and placement.

Integrate the colors of fire—red, orange, brick, or vermilion—into the heart of the garden. Red charges us and helps us feel warm, both emotionally and physically. Stay away from blue, the color of ice, in your winter's garden.

Warmth is also promoted by using triangular shapes, such as the peaked roof of a birdhouse. A triangle is the shape of a flame and can add warmth to a dreary, cold day. Conversely, avoid vertical lines or rectangles in the heart of this garden.

Objects that invite motion, such as a bird or squirrel feeder, or objects that actually move, such as a kinetic sculpture, emit an energy appropriate in winter. I remember one December day when my son and I went to a New York Jets football game. The temperature was below zero, but the fans were sitting and watching the game as if it were a warm autumn day. The stadium was filled with people jumping out of their seats, flailing their arms in excitement, and generally moving around almost as much as the players on the field. No matter how fascinating it would be, I doubt anyone would come out in frigid weather to view a championship chess match. Motion warms us actually and visually.

Add to the warmth of your winter's garden by using full-spectrum lightbulbs in the outdoor fixtures. If there isn't a spotlight already mounted nearby, purchase one that can be plugged into an outdoor socket and position it to shine on the heart. To counteract the darkness during winter, light up the world surrounding your heart during the evening hours.

Suggestions for a Focal Point

Birdhouse
Dried corn in a wheelbarrow
Snow people
Sundial
Polished stone sculpture
Wood sculpture
Ceramic sculpture

Suggestions for Plants as the Focal Point

Red-twig dogwood
Willow
Cedar of Lebanon
Deodar cedar
Madrone
Harry Lauder's walking stick
Spruce
Clipped holly

Tip: To promote strong color in the dogwood and willows, cut them to the ground at regular intervals, such as every two to three years, depending on their rate of growth. In addition, cut back one-third of the branches to ground level every year.

PLANTS AND GROUND COVERING

If there are withered or dead plants in this garden, either trim them back or remove them. Do not leave dead stalks or drooping pods hanging from vines to remind you of endings. The winter's garden should cheer us, not remind us of the mortality of all living things.

Consider foliage as a catalyst for visual activity in the garden. Use a hedge as a structure for draping tiny white lights to warm the area visually. A lawn, devoid of the full, rich green of spring, can become a blanket upon which you scatter treats for wildlife. Seeing a squirrel scamper across the lawn or a bird swoop down from the skies to nab the treats on the ground is a way to bring life to a still scene.

A winter's garden gives you a reason to go outside. While it is fun to create, the measure of its success lies in its ability to entertain and energize while you are confined inside. It is lighthearted, joyful, and long-lasting during the time of year when clothes are heavy, food is hearty, and days are short.

17

Retirement Garden

Gratification

Benevolence

Familiarity

Comfort

W hen children and careers have blossomed and come to fruition or when a home has reached a comfort zone and requires no further major change, it is time to turn to the never-ending pleasures of gardening. We may have retired from a job, but we never need to retire from the benefits of cultivating nature. Gardening can be deeply satisfying later in life. In a garden we are both the nurturer and the nurtured.

Aging is often associated only with loss—namely, an empty nest, the loss of parents and friends, diminished eyesight and hearing, or limited flexibility. While we cannot halt some of these conditions, we can facilitate experiences that force us to be aware and understanding of our limitations. A garden allows us to experience renewal, which is a vital part of a contented living experience.

Even though our reflexes may not be as fast nor our senses as acute as they were in the past, we are often rewarded with additional wisdom and patience as we age. At the end of her life, the French author Colette's mother refused to leave her home to move in with her daughter, who could care for her. Her mother knew full well that staying at home would shorten her life. She based her decision on her desire to see the bloom of a cactus that flowered only once every seven years. Perhaps our understanding of life's secrets is deepened and enriched as we dance through time.

Nevertheless, it would be foolhardy not to plan for potentially special needs. Although many of us will not be confined to a wheelchair or need the use of a walker, a productive, outdoor activity space for later years should be barrier-free. Clearing away obstacles, selecting an easy-to-reach location, and including features to increase stability will help us enjoy gardening in our retirement years.

A retirement garden is characterized by elements with heightened sensory appeal. Brilliant colors, pungent fragrances, and shapes with sharp definition are easier to experience with senses dimming with age. The clearer and more definitive each sensory experience is, the easier it will be to appreciate. Appropriate plantings for this garden include flowers with robust fragrances, such as gardenias; leaves with crisp, definite shapes, such as those of a holly; and plants with distinctive colors, such as begonias, whose vibrant red bristles against its green leaves.

One of the pleasures associated with aging is that we have fewer and fewer *shoulds* in our lives. We can participate in as much or as little gardening as we like. A retirement garden never requires a vigilance that if neglected would cause harm to the plants. We plant what our soil and climate want to nurture. We plant vegetation that is not fussy or requires special, intensive care to thrive. As the ancient sage Lao Tzu writes:

There are those who want to control the world by action
But I see that they cannot succeed . . .
Therefore the sage
avoids the extremes,
avoids the extravagant
and avoids the excessive.

Our last garden gives us an opportunity to be involved while letting go. It gives back more to us than we are required to contribute. It is, in fact, a gift we give ourselves as the years wane.

PLACEMENT

A narrow, raised bed placed against a house, next to a fence, or along the perimeter of a porch or deck is ideal for a retirement garden. Since visual sharpness and contrast are important considerations in this garden, a high structure for a backdrop serves as a foil for a clear view of the plantings. Locate this garden close to the house. Many times the house itself can be used as a supporting wall.

house wall
or fence

A high structure serves as an excellent backdrop.

The benefits of the narrow depth of the raised bed include easy access and the avoidance of kneeling to plant or prune. Moreover, a higher bed brings the sight, smell, and touch of the garden closer to the eyes, nose, and hands.

For people who do not have an outdoor space, a retirement garden can be a planter on a windowsill, a terra cotta pot on a kitchen table, or a bowl on a bedside table.

Suggestions for Placement

Outside the front or back door
Along the outside of the house
On a windowsill
In the center of a kitchen table

Locate your retirement garden in a highly visible place that is convenient for you.

EDGES AND SHAPE

The edges of a retirement garden will be determined by the length of the wall supporting the earth. If you create a freestanding stepped wall, place it along one side of a prominent pathway. The borders will be determined by the frame supporting this garden.

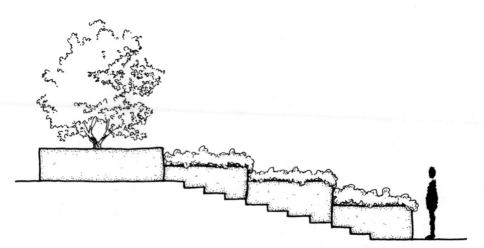

Raised planters at entry stairs

Suggestions for Edges

Brick
Concrete
Clay/adobe
Railroad ties
Stone
Stockade fencing

PATHWAYS

Be sure that the passageway is at least 33 inches wide. My vital 83-year-old father-in-law slipped on a wet concrete walkway on his way to the pool at his complex. His broken ankle not only inconvenienced him, but also rendered him immobile because the doors to his bathroom and side yard were too narrow for either a wheelchair or a walker. Had the builder of his subdivision provided wider openings for access doors, my father-in-law would have been more mobile and probably more cheerful during his convalescence.

Even though many of us will never be confined to a wheelchair, most of us will be larger in girth during our retirement years than we had previously been. We need somewhat more space because of this and because we cannot maneuver our bodies quite as dexterously as we once did. The design and planning of the pathway should accommodate our physical needs.

The shape of the path to the retirement garden will be determined by where it is located. Because this garden requires retaining walls, it is easier to build this garden with straight lines. Therefore, to help give the feel of a curved passage, which feng shui rightly states is a preferred shape, stagger the front wall so that it takes on the spirit of a curve. If the path is straight, stagger the planters to break up the straight line. A long, straight path encourages visitors to walk faster; therefore, we need to encourage dawdling and strolling by softening the straight line of the path into a visual curve.

The edge and pathway of a retirement garden will most likely follow preexisting routes surrounding a home. Inside the home, make sure the planter or pot is accessible and easy to reach. Be sure there is enough room to approach the container with hands filled with clippers and a vase for placing cuttings. An unobstructed windowsill or the center of a dining table are examples of locations that suit this indoor scape.

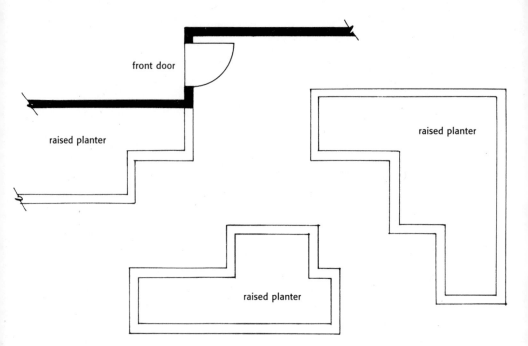

The staggered placement of planters fosters the illusion of a curved line.

THE HEART, OR FOCUS, OF THE GARDEN

One of the most sensual of all gardening delights is a bed of herbs. Using fresh herbs to prepare our meals can add healthful, delectable nuances to our daily fare. The flavoring and seasoning they contribute have no culinary equivalent. A sprig of freshly cut parsley can turn a dreary mound of mashed potatoes into a visual delight; a few long stems of chive can add a gourmet touch to a pale, white fish fillet. Indeed, by planting herbs in a retirement garden, we can liven up our dishes as well as our lives. The countless varieties of herbs can do more than season our favorite meals. Herbs can also add beauty to our lives when used in arrangements of dried flowers and leaves or when used by themselves as adornment.

Herbs have other important characteristics. They are relatively inexpensive to buy and to grow. We reap the rewards almost immediately after planting them. Only small quantities are needed for seasoning, and invariably there is enough in even an immature plant to supply an adequate amount.

Herbs are relatively disease- and pest-free and tend to be hardy. Many live a long time. Thyme and sage seem to last forever in milder climates. And even in the heat of summer, my basil plant, placed under the shadowing screen of a tree, grows and grows and grows. Even though many herbs are adaptable and hardy, they are generally happiest in sunny, dry conditions with well-drained soil.

Suggestions for Herbs Suitable for Growing Outdoors

Parsley
Basil
Chive
Lemongrass
Verbena
Thyme
Rosemary

Suggestions for Herbs Suitable for Arranging

Sea lavendar
Rose (older varieties)
Bells of Ireland
Strawflower
Bachelor's button
Hop-plant
Hydrangea
Chinese lantern
Sea holly
Bear's-breech
Baby's breath

The shape of a retirement garden should be higher in the back and lower in the front. Plant the potentially tallest herbs behind the smaller varieties.

Taller Herbs for the Backdrop

Rosemary (upright variety)
Lavender
Scented geraniums
Caraway

Sage
Fennel
Dill

Medium-Size Herbs for the Center

Chive
Basil
Coriander
Tarragon

Low-Growing Herbs for the Front Edge

Thyme
Prostrate rosemary
Chamomile
Verbena
Mint

No matter which herbs you choose, the payback can be vast. A new favorite dish may become pesto sauce made with fresh basil. Whether mint from your garden is infused in a glass of lemonade, or a few leaves of thyme are added to a pot of simmering pinto beans, the herbs in the retirement garden will flavor your foods in delightful and sometimes unexpected ways.

OTHER PLANTS

Adorn the sides of this garden with large, colorful flowers. They should be higher than the herbs, but not higher than the backdrop. Select plants that are appropriate for the height and color of your background: orange lilies against a white clapboard New England home, black-eyed Susans in front of a Midwestern Tudor home, or blue daisies against a pale lemon stucco cottage.

Having a home filled with the colorful design of freshly cut flowers or ornamental leaves can be inspirational and mood elevating. Refer to the color plant chart in the back of the book to select plants that would be best suited to your color scheme.

Flowers with Large Blooms

Lily of the Nile
Iris varieties

Daylily
Camellia
Gardenia varieties

There is no reason to be disconnected from the vitality of nature at any point in our life. By focusing on accessibility and convenience, we furnish ourselves with a touchstone for life. A retirement garden represents, in miniature, the cycles of life and our dependence on all things. It is truly the spirit of the Tao which reminds us that to stay connected is to be alive.

18

INVOCATIONS FOR SUCCESS

"Miracles happen, not in opposition to Nature, but in opposition to what we know of Nature."

St. Augustine

Every molecule is linked to all others in an endless chain of connections. From the moment we assume a physical form, we are caressed by the cosmos. Each universe mirrors all others, and whatever we may want exists already in time and place. Whether the picture is microscopic or macroscopic, the building blocks are the same. Connection, balance, and energy are the keys to life.

Plant a rose and learn to love. Sit by a rock, and strength will infuse your spirit. Smell freshly cut grass, and learn that paring away strengthens the opportunity for new growth. These insights are gifts that never fade and cannot be taken from you.

Till, plant, arrange nature's objects, and in doing so, the earth will become your ally. The message is the action. In life, as in a garden, you reap what you sow.

Conceiving a special garden can create a vortex around which actualization can dawn. Inside our dwellings there are fewer opportunities to furnish ourselves with specific locations that satisfy individual needs, desires, and hopes. In fact, often the opposite is true. A bedroom frequently is used as a dressing room, an entertainment center, and a secondary office. How rest, relaxation, and sleep can be honored and dignified in the midst of this cacophony of themes is anyone's best guess. Conversely, outside in nature, we have the luxury of sequestering an area for one special activity. Choosing a garden is often the first step in interpreting priorities.

Which seed is to be planted is for you to determine. Can the concept of fertility stimulate you to unleash a flood of ideas or feelings? Will a tranquil spot for meditation provide the solitude necessary to remove the roadblocks that obscure your contentment? Will a retirement garden allow you to continue nurturing? The answers are not necessarily to be wrung out like water from a sponge. Unearthing the solutions lies not in the destination, but in the passage. Let intuition guide you, and let the process of beginning be enough.

The difficulty with all styles of contemporary life is that they involve loss of intimacy with the natural spirit or order of this world. As biological creatures we are meant to be reflected and inscribed in the cosmic order. Instead, our lives are encircled with barriers that separate us from nature.

Protecting ourselves from experiencing anything unpleasant is a double-edged sword. While artificial warmth stifles winter's icy sting, it also quells the need to move about and often inhibits the desire to go outside. To experience epiphanies we need to unearth channels within us, and a garden is often the ideal place for this quest.

Outdoor spaces are often not infused with many cultural requirements. We are free to invent and create whatever we choose. Unlike making a decision to use an extra bedroom for exercising or meditation, starting with no interior walls gives us the options to have it all.

And finally, by growing an outdoor room, we give birth to ritual. Our choices emanate from our past, connect us to the present, and design the potential for the future.

The gardens described in this book are meant to link us with the spirit of the earth as well as with our spiritual intentions. Some gardens are informal; others are ceremonial. All are intended to stimulate us to investigate the forces within ourselves, as well as in nature. To direct human energies into the essence of self and self-lessness and to provide a golden thread with which to weave a dream, a garden expresses our heartfelt desires and conjoins us with the soul of life.

It is up to you to grow a future.

PLANT MATERIAL	ASSOCIATION WITH ELEMENTS/SHAPES						PROPERTIES		
	FIRE/TRIANGLE	EARTH/SQUARE	METAL/ROUND	WATER/CURVED/WAVY	WOOD/RECTANGLE	WEEPING SHAPE	ATTRACTS BUTTERFLIES	ATTRACTS BIRDS	DEER-RESISTANT
TREES									
Acacia (*Acacia*)								■	■
Alder (*Alnus*)								■	
Arborvitae (*Thuja*)	■								
Ash (*Fraxinus*)	■								
Beech (*Fagus*)	■								
Birch (*Betula*)	■							■	
Bottlebrush (*Callistemon*)									■
Chaste Tree (*Vitex*)							■		
Chinaberry (*Melia*)								■	■
Citrus (*Citrus*)							■	■	
Crab Apple (*Malus*)				■				■	
Cypress (*Cupressus*)	□				□				
Deodar Cedar (*Cedrus*)				■		■			
Dogwood (*Cornus*)				■				■	
Elderberry (*Sambucus*)								■	
Elm (*Ulmus*)								■	
Eucalyptus (*Eucalyptus*)									■
Fig (*Ficus carica*)								■	
Fir (*Abies*)								■	■
Ginkgo (*Ginkgo*)	■								
Hackberry (*Celtis*)								■	
Horse Chestnut (*Aesculus*)							■		
Juniper (*Juniperus*)	□				□				
Larch (*Larix*)								■	
Loquat (*Eriobotrya*)								■	
Madrone (*Arbutus*)							■		■
Magnolia (*Magnolia*)	■								
Maple (*Acer*)		□						■	■
Mimosa (*Albizia*)								■	■
Monkey Puzzle (*Araucaria*)				■					

KEY   ■ = all species   □ = some species, varieties, or cultivars only

PLANT MATERIAL	ASSOCIATION WITH ELEMENTS/SHAPES						PROPERTIES		
	FIRE/TRIANGLE	EARTH/SQUARE	METAL/ROUND	WATER/CURVED/WAVY	WOOD/RECTANGLE	WEEPING SHAPE	ATTRACTS BUTTERFLIES	ATTRACTS BIRDS	DEER-RESISTANT
TREES (CONTINUED)									
Mountain Ash (*Sorbus*)								■	
Oak (*Quercus*)			■	□				■	
Paloverde (*Cercidium*)								■	
Pine (*Pinus*)	□		□					■	■
Purple-Leaved Plum (*Prunus*)				■					
Redwood (*Sequoia*)	■								
Smoke Tree (*Cotinus*)									■
Spanish Dagger (*Yucca*)	■			■					
Spruce (*Picea*)	■							■	■
Sweet Gum (*Liquidambar*)	■								■
Tanbark Oak (*Lithocarpus*)									■
Tulip Tree (*Liriodendron*)	■								
Willow (*Salix*)	■		■	■		■	■		
Willow Myrtle (*Agonis*)						■			
SHRUBS									
Abelia (*Abelia*)							■		
Acacia (*Acacia*)								■	
Barberry (*Berberis*)									■
Beauty Bush (*Kolkwitzia*)							■		
Bleeding Heart (*Dicentra*)						■			
Boxwood (*Buxus*)		■							■
Butterfly Bush (*Buddleia*)							■	■	■
Chinese Lantern (*Abutilon*)						■			
Coffeeberry (*Rhamnus*)							■		
Cotoneaster (*Cotoneaster*)									■
Crown Imperial (*Fritillaria*)						■			
Currant, Gooseberry (*Ribes*)							■	■	■
Escallonia (*Escallonia*)							■		
Euonymous (*Euonymous*)		■						■	
Firethorn (*Pyracantha*)								■	
Flowering Quince (*Chaenomeles*)								■	

PLANT MATERIAL	ASSOCIATION WITH ELEMENTS/SHAPES						PROPERTIES		
	FIRE/TRIANGLE	EARTH/SQUARE	METAL/ROUND	WATER/CURVED/WAVY	WOOD/RECTANGLE	WEEPING SHAPE	ATTRACTS BUTTERFLIES	ATTRACTS BIRDS	DEER-RESISTANT
SHRUBS (CONTINUED)									
Forsythia (*Forsythia*)									■
Fuchsia (*Fuchsia*)	■					■		■	
Goldenrod (*Solidago*)								■	
Grevillea (*Grevillea*)								■	■
Heath (*Erica*)								■	
Hebe (*Hebe*)			■						
Holly (*Ilex*)	■				■				
Honeysuckle (*Lonicera*)			■	■		■	■	■	
Hydrangea (*Hydrangea*)			■	■					
Japanese Aralia (*Fatsia*)			■						
Jasmine (*Jasminum*)									■
Juneberry (*Amelanchier*)								■	
Juniper (*Juniperus*)		□	□						■
Lavender (*Lavandula*)							■		
Lavender Starflower (*Grewia*)							■		
Leucothoe (*Leucothoe*)									■
Lilac (*Syringa*)							■		
Manzanita (*Arctostaphylos*)							■	■	
Oregon Grape (*Mahonia*)								■	■
Pineapple Guava (*Feijoa*)								■	
Privet (*Ligustrum*)								■	
Rhododendron (*Rhododendron*)							■		
Rockrose (*Cistus*)		■							■
Rose (*Rosa*)		□							
Rosemary (*Rosmarinus*)							■	■	■
Sage (*Salvia*)									■
Silk Tassel (*Garrya*)						■		■	
Silverberry (*Elaeagnus*)								■	
Snowball (*Viburnum*)			■	■				■	
Snowdrop (*Galanthus*)						■			
Spirea (*Spiraea*)		■							
Sumac (*Rhus*)								■	■

PLANT MATERIAL	ASSOCIATION WITH ELEMENTS/SHAPES						PROPERTIES		
	FIRE/TRIANGLE	EARTH/SQUARE	METAL/ROUND	WATER/CURVED/WAVY	WOOD/RECTANGLE	WEEPING SHAPE	ATTRACTS BUTTERFLIES	ATTRACTS BIRDS	DEER-RESISTANT
SHRUBS (CONTINUED)									
Tea Tree (*Leptospermum*)									■
Toyon (*Heteromeles*)								■	
Tree Mallow (*Lavatera*)				■					
Weigela (*Weigela*)							■		
Wild Lilac (*Ceanothus*)							■	■	■
Wormwood (*Artemisia*)		■	■						
Yew (*Taxus*)		■				□			■
ANNUALS AND PERENNIALS									
Aster (*Aster*)							■		
Bearded Iris (*Iris*)									■
Beardtongue (*Penstemon*)							■	■	
Belladonna Lily (*Amaryllis*)	■								
Bird-of-Paradise (*Strelitzia*)	■								
Black-Eyed Susan (*Rudbeckia*)	■								
Blanketflower (*Gaillardia*)							■	■	
Bleeding Heart (*Dicentra*)								■	
Borage (*Borago*)							■		
Bugbane (*Cimicifuga*)					■				
Buttercup (*Ranunculus*)							■		
California Poppy (*Eschscholzia*)		■							
Calla Lily (*Zantedeschia*)		■							
Candytuft (*Iberis*)							■		
Cardinal Flower (*Lobelia*)				■					
Catnip (*Nepeta*)									■
Century Plant (*Agave*)	■								
Chive (*Allium*)			■	■					
Cinquefoil (*Potentilla*)				■					
Clarkia (*Clarkia*)								■	
Columbine (*Aquilegia*)							■	■	
Coralbells (*Heuchera*)							■		
Coreopsis (*Coreopsis*)							■	■	

PLANT MATERIAL	ASSOCIATION WITH ELEMENTS/SHAPES						PROPERTIES		
	FIRE/TRIANGLE	EARTH/SQUARE	METAL/ROUND	WATER/CURVED/WAVY	WOOD/RECTANGLE	WEEPING SHAPE	ATTRACTS BUTTERFLIES	ATTRACTS BIRDS	DEER-RESISTANT
ANNUALS AND PERENNIALS (CONTINUED)									
Cosmos (*Cosmos*)							■	■	
Daffodil (*Narcissus*)									■
Delphinium (*Delphinium*)							■		
False Solomon's Seal (*Smilacina*)				■					
False Spirea (*Astilbe*)									■
Ferns (many varieties)									■
Fleabane (*Erigeron*)							■		
Forget-Me-Not (*Myosotis*)									■
Fountain Grass (*Pennisetum*)	■								
Foxglove (*Digitalis*)								■	■
Garden Phlox (*Phlox*)			■	■					
Geranium (*Pelargonium*)				■				■	
Ginger Lily (*Hedychium*)					■				
Globeflower (*Trollius*)			■	■					
Globe Thistle (*Echinops*)			■	■					
Gloriosa Daisy (*Rudbeckia*)							■		
Goldenrod (*Solidago*)				■					
Hart's-Tongue Fern (*Phyllitis*)				■					
Hollyhock (*Alcea*)								■	
Horsemint (*Monarda*)								■	
Hummingbird's Trumpet (*Zauschneria*)								■	
Iris (*Iris*)	■			■					
Jupiter's Beard (*Centranthus*)							■		
Kaffir Lily (*Clivia*)									■
Knotweed (*Polygonum*)					■				
Lamb's Ears (*Stachys*)		■							
Larkspur (*Delphinium*)				■			■	■	
Lavender (*Lavandula*)									■
Lavender Cotton (*Santolina*)		■							■
Lemon Balm (*Melissa*)				■					
Lily of the Nile (*Agapanthus*)							■		

PLANT MATERIAL	ASSOCIATION WITH ELEMENTS/SHAPES						PROPERTIES		
	FIRE/TRIANGLE	EARTH/SQUARE	METAL/ROUND	WATER/CURVED/WAVY	WOOD/RECTANGLE	WEEPING SHAPE	ATTRACTS BUTTERFLIES	ATTRACTS BIRDS	DEER-RESISTANT
ANNUALS AND PERENNIALS (CONTINUED)									
Lion's-Tail (*Leonotis*)								■	■
Loosestrife (*Lysimachia*)				■	■				
Lupine (*Lupinus*)	■								
Mallow (*Malva*)				■					
Mint (*Mentha*)									■
Monkshood (*Aconitum*)									■
New Zealand Flax (*Phormium tenax*)	■								
Nicotiana (*Nicotiana*)								■	
Oregano (*Origanum*)							■		
Oswego Tea (*Monarda*)									■
Oxalis (*Oxalis*)				■					
Peony (*Paeonia*)				■					
Pink (*Dianthus*)				■			■		
Plantain Lily (*Hosta*)			■	■					
Poppy (*Papaver*)									■
Purple Coneflower (*Echinacea*)							■		
Red-Hot Poker (*Kniphofia*)									■
Rodgersia (*Rodgersia*)		■	■	■					
Rose Campion (*Lychnis*)									■
Sage (*Salvia*)							■		
Sea Holly (*Eryngium*)	■						■		
Shasta Daisy (*Chrysanthemum*)							■		
Snapdragon (*Antirrhinum*)							■	■	
Spiderflower (*Cleome*)								■	
Sunflower (*Helianthus*)								■	
Sweet Alyssum (*Lobularia*)							■		
Sweet Pea (*Lathyrus*)							■		
Thrift (*Armeria*)							■		
Tuberous Begonia (*Begonia*)									■

PLANT MATERIAL	ASSOCIATION WITH ELEMENTS/SHAPES						PROPERTIES		
	FIRE/TRIANGLE	EARTH/SQUARE	METAL/ROUND	WATER/CURVED/WAVY	WOOD/RECTANGLE	WEEPING SHAPE	ATTRACTS BUTTERFLIES	ATTRACTS BIRDS	DEER-RESISTANT
ANNUALS AND PERENNIALS (CONTINUED)									
Verbena (*Verbena*)	■	■					■		
Windflower (*Anemone*)				■					■
Wormwood (*Artemisia*)									■
Yarrow (*Achillea*)	■	■					■		
VINES AND GROUND COVERS									
Blue Star Creeper (*Laurentia*)									■
Cape Honeysuckle (*Tecomaria*)									■
Cardinal Climber (*Ipomoea*)								■	
Carolina Yellow Jessamine (*Gelsemium*)									■
Chinese Wisteria (*Wisteria*)				■		■			
Clematis (*Clematis*)								■	■
Flame Vine (*Pyrostegia*)								■	
Jasmine (*Jasminum*)									■
Manzanita (*Arctostaphylos*)									■
Trumpet Vine (*Campsis*)								■	
Wild Strawberry (*Fragaria*)									■
Wonga-Wonga Vine (*Pandorea*)									■

APPENDIX B   COLOR PLANT CHARTS

When planning your garden, you can incorporate color in a variety of ways. In addition to flowers and fruit, consider the variety of colors in foliage. Consult your local landscape professional for the varieties available in your area.

PLANT MATERIAL	COLOR			
	GRAY	BRONZE/RED	YELLOW/GOLD	BLUE
TREES				
American Arborvitae (*Thuja*)			□	
Arizona Cypress (*Cupressus*)	■			
Black Locust (*Robinia*)		■		
Colorado Blue Spruce (*Picea*)				□
Dracaena (*Cordyline*)		□		
Eastern Redbud (*Cercis*)		□		
Eucalyptus (*Eucalyptus*)	□			□
European Beech (*Fagus*)		□		
False Cypress (*Chamaecyparis*)				□
Honey Locust (*Gleditsia*)			■	
Japanese Maple (*Acer*)		□	■	
Juniper (*Juniperus*)	□			□
Smoke Tree (*Cotinus*)		■		
SHRUBS				
Bush Germander (*Teucrium*)	■			
Bush Morning-Glory (*Convolvulus*)	■			
English Yew (*Taxus*)			□	
False Cypress (*Chamaecyparis*)			□	□
Filbert (*Corylus*)		■		
Hummingbird's Trumpet (*Zauschneria*)	■			
Juniper (*Juniperus*)	□		□	
Lancewood (*Pseudopanax*)		■		
Lavender Cotton (*Santolina*)	■			
Mexican Bush Sage (*Salvia*)	■			■
Nevin Mahonia (*Mahonia*)	■			
Oriental Arborvitae (*Platycladus*)			□	
Pimelea (*Pimelea*)	■			

KEY   ■ = all contain this color   □ = some contain this color

PLANT MATERIAL	COLOR	GRAY	BRONZE/RED	YELLOW/GOLD	BLUE
Shrubs (continued)					
Privet (*Ligustrum*)				□	
Purple Hop Bush (*Dodonaea*)			■		
Saltbush (*Atriplex*)		■			
Silver Tree (*Leucodendron*)		■			
Silverberry (*Elaeagnus*)		■			
Texas Ranger (*Leucophyllum*)		■			
Wormwood (*Artemisia*)		■			
Annuals and Perennials					
Artichoke (*Cynara*)		■			
Bowles' Golden Grass (*Milium*)				■	
Canna (*Canna*)			□		
Carpet Bugle (*Ajuga*)			□		
Cotyledon (*Cotyledon*)		■			
Crete Dittany (*Origanum*)		■			
Crown Pink (*Lychnis*)		■			
Cushionbush (*Calocephalus*)		■			
Dudleya (*Dudleya*)		■			
Dusty Miller (*Senecio*)		■			
Euryops (*Euryops*)		■			
False Spirea (*Astilbe*)			□		
Fescue (*Festuca*)				■	■
Floss Flower (*Ageratum*)					■
Fountain Grass (*Pennisetum*)			□		
Lamb's Ears (*Stachys*)		■			
Larkspur (*Delphinium*)			■		■
Lavender (*Lavandula*)		□			
Lily of the Nile (*Agapanthus*)					■
Lupine (*Lupinus*)					■
Morning Glory (*Ipomoea*)			■		■
New Zealand Flax (*Phormium*)			□		
Pincushion Flower (*Scabiosa*)					■
Snow-in-Summer (*Cerastium*)		■			

PLANT MATERIAL	COLOR	GRAY	BRONZE/RED	YELLOW/GOLD	BLUE
ANNUALS AND PERENNIALS (CONTINUED)					
Stock (*Matthiola*)		▓			
Stonecrop (*Sedum*)		☐			
Velvet Centaurea (*Centaurea*)	▓				
Yarrow (*Achillea*)	▓				

Fruits and Berries

Colorful fruits and berries add bright spots of color. As always, consult an extension service, a garden club, or a local landscape professional to determine the varieties that are best for your region.

PLANT MATERIAL	BERRY/FRUIT COLOR								
	WHITE	PURPLE	PINK	RED	ORANGE	YELLOW	SALMON/CORAL	BLUE	BLACK
TREES									
Chinese Flame Tree (*Koelreuteria*)							■		
Crab Apple (*Malus*)				■					
Dogwood (*Cornus*)				■	■				
Elderberry (*Sambucus*)				■				■	■
Filbert (*Corylus*)						■			
Hawthorn (*Crataegus*)				■					
Holly (*Ilex*)				■					
Lillypilly (*Acmena*)	■	■	■						
Loquat (*Eriobotrya*)					■	■			
Peppertree (*Schinus*)				■					
Strawberry Tree (*Arbutus*)				■					
Toyon (*Heteromeles*)				■					
SHRUBS									
Barberry (*Berberis*)		■		■			■	■	
Beauty Bush (*Kolkwitzia*)			■						
Beautyberry (*Callicarpa*)		■							
Chinese Photinia (*Photinia*)				■					
Cotoneaster (*Cotoneaster*)				■					
Currant, Gooseberry (*Ribes*)				■		■			■
Firethorn (*Pyracantha*)				■					
Honeysuckle (*Lonicera*)		■		■					
Indian Hawthorne (*Raphiolepis*)								■	
Natal Plum (*Carissa*)				■					
Oregon Grape (*Mahonia*)				■				■	■
Pomegranate (*Punica*)				■					

PLANT MATERIAL	BERRY/FRUIT COLOR	WHITE	PURPLE	PINK	RED	ORANGE	YELLOW	SALMON/CORAL	BLUE	BLACK
SHRUBS (CONTINUED)										
Silverberry (*Elaeagnus*)					■	■		■		
Skyflower (*Duranta repens*)							■			
Snowberry (*Symphoricarpos*)		■		■						
Staghorn Sumac (*Rhus*)					■					

BLOOMS

Of course, blooms are special favorites for adding color to your garden. In the chart that follows, the annuals and perennials add color and are grouped by their performance in each of the four seasons.

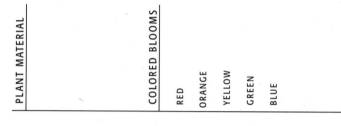

PLANT MATERIAL	COLORED BLOOMS				
	RED	ORANGE	YELLOW	GREEN	BLUE
SPRING					
Annuals					
African Daisy (*Arctotis*)	■	■	■		
Bachelor's Button (*Centaurea*)	■				■
California Poppy (*Eschscholzia*)	■	■	■		
Candytuft (*Iberis*)	■				
Cape Marigold (*Dimorphotheca*)		■	■		
Cineraria (*Senecio*)	■				■
Clarkia (*Clarkia*)	■				
Forget-Me-Not (*Myosotis*)					■
Iceland Poppy (*Papaver*)	■	■	■		
Nasturtium (*Tropaeolum*)	■	■	■		
Nemesia (*Nemesia*)	■	■	■		■
Pansy (*Viola*)	■	■	■		■
Petunia (*Petunia*)	■	■	■		■
Pot Marigold (*Calendula*)		■	■		
Snapdragon (*Antirrhinum*)	■	■	■		
Stock (*Matthiola*)	■				
Sweet Pea (*Lathyrus*)	■				■
Perennials					
African Daisy (*Arctotis*)		■			
Basket-of-Gold (*Aurinia*)		■			
Beardtongue (*Penstemon*)	■				■
Bellflower (*Campanula*)					■
Bergenia (*Bergenia*)	■				
Bleeding Heart (*Dicentra*)	■				
Calla Lily (*Zantedeschia*)	■				

PLANT MATERIAL	COLORED BLOOMS	RED	ORANGE	YELLOW	GREEN	BLUE
Perennials (continued)						
Candytuft (*Iberis*)		■				
Columbine (*Aquilegia*)		■	■	■		■
Coralbells (*Heuchera*)		■			■	
Coreopsis (*Coreopsis*)		■	■			
Daylily (*Hemerocallis*)		■	■			
Gazania (*Gazania*)		■	■			
Geranium (*Pelargonium*)		■				
Hellebore (*Helleborus*)					■	
Iceland Poppy (*Papaver*)		■	■			
Iris (*Iris*)				■	■	■
Jupiter's Beard (*Centranthus*)		■				
Pansy (*Viola*)		■				■
Peony (*Paeonia*)		■	■			
Peruvian Lily (*Alstroemeria*)		■	■			
Primrose (*Primula*)		■				■
Red-Hot Poker (*Kniphofia*)		■	■	■		
Spurge (*Euphorbia*)					■	
Sweet William (*Dianthus*)		■				■
Wake-Robin (*Trillium*)		■				

SUMMER

PLANT MATERIAL	COLORED BLOOMS	RED	ORANGE	YELLOW	GREEN	BLUE
Annuals						
African Daisy (*Arctotis*)		■	■	■		
Aster (*Aster*)		■				■
Bachelor's Button (*Centaurea*)		■				■
Bells of Ireland (*Moluccella*)					■	
Blanketflower (*Gaillardia*)		■	■			
California Poppy (*Eschscholzia*)		■	■	■		
Candytuft (*Iberis*)		■				
Chrysanthemum (*Chrysanthemum*)		■	■	■		
Cockscomb (*Celosia*)			■	■		
Coleus (*Coleus*)		■	■	■	■	
Dahlia (*Dahlia*)		■	■	■		

PLANT MATERIAL	COLORED BLOOMS				
	RED	ORANGE	YELLOW	GREEN	BLUE
Annuals (continued)					
Forget-Me-Not (*Myosotis*)					■
Iceland Poppy (*Papaver*)	■	■	■		
Impatiens (*Impatiens*)	■	■			
Lobelia (*Lobelia*)	■				■
Marigold (*Tagetes*)		■	■		
Mignonette (*Reseda*)			■	■	
Monkey Flower (*Mimulus*)	■		■		
Morning Glory (*Ipomoea*)					■
Nicotiana (*Nicotiana*)	■			■	
Pansy (*Viola*)	■	■	■		■
Petunia (*Petunia*)	■	■	■		■
Snapdragon (*Antirrhinum*)	■	■	■		
Strawflower (*Helichrysum*)	■	■	■		
Tuberous (*Begonia*)	■	■			
Verbena (*Verbena*)	■				■
Zinnia (*Zinnia*)	■	■	■	■	
Perennials					
Aster (*Aster*)	■				■
Avens (*Geum*)	■	■	■		
Beardtongue (*Penstemon*)	■				■
Black-Eyed Susan (*Rudbeckia*)	■	■	■		
Blanketflower (*Gaillardia*)	■	■	■		
Bleeding Heart (*Dicentra*)	■				
Calla Lily (*Zantedeschia*)	■		■		
Canna (*Canna*)	■	■	■		
Chrysanthemum (*Chrysanthemum*)	■	■			
Columbine (*Aquilegia*)	■		■		■
Coralbells (*Heuchera*)	■			■	
Daylily (*Hemerocallis*)	■	■	■		
False Spirea (*Astilbe*)	■				
Geranium (*Pelargonium*)	■		■		
Globeflower (*Trollius*)		■	■		
Golden Marguerite (*Anthemis*)		■	■		

PLANT MATERIAL	COLORED BLOOMS	RED	ORANGE	YELLOW	GREEN	BLUE

Perennials (continued)

PLANT MATERIAL	RED	ORANGE	YELLOW	GREEN	BLUE
Hollyhock (*Alcea*)	■				
Iris (*Iris*)	■	■	■	■	■
Jupiter's Beard (*Centranthus*)	■				
Peruvian Lily (*Alstroemeria*)	■	■	■		
Phlox (*Phlox*)	■				■
Pink (*Dianthus*)	■	■	■		
Primrose (*Primula*)	■	■	■		■
Purple Coneflower (*Echinacea*)	■				
Red-Hot Poker (*Kniphofia*)	■	■	■		
Sneezeweed (*Helenium*)	■	■	■		
Stonecrop (*Sedum*)	■		■		
Verbena (*Verbena*)	■				■
Yarrow (*Achillea*)	■	■	■		

AUTUMN

Annuals

PLANT MATERIAL	RED	ORANGE	YELLOW	GREEN	BLUE
Begonia (*Begonia*)	■	■	■		
Chrysanthemum (*Chrysanthemum*)	■	■	■		
Cosmos (*Cosmos*)	■	■	■		
Dahlia (*Dahlia*)	■	■	■		
Flowering Cabbage (*Brassica*)	■			■	
Marigold (*Tagetes*)	■	■	■		
Nasturtium (*Tropaeolum*)	■	■	■		
Phlox (*Phlox*)	■		■		
Portulaca (*Portulaca*)	■	■	■		
Pot Marigold (*Calendula*)		■	■		
Sunflower (*Helianthus*)		■	■		
Verbena (*Verbena*)	■				■
Zinnia (*Zinnia*)	■	■		■	

Perennials

PLANT MATERIAL	RED	ORANGE	YELLOW	GREEN	BLUE
Aster (*Aster*)	■				■
Black-Eyed Susan (*Rudbeckia*)	■	■	■		
Blanketflower (*Gaillardia*)	■	■	■		

PLANT MATERIAL	COLORED BLOOMS				
	RED	ORANGE	YELLOW	GREEN	BLUE
Perennials *(continued)*					
Bleeding Heart (*Dicentra*)	■				
Canna (*Canna*)	■	■	■		
Chrysanthemum (*Chrysanthemum*)	■	■	■		
Coreopsis (*Coreopsis*)	■	■	■		
Cranesbill (*Pelargonium*)					■
Daylily (*Hemerocallis*)	■	■	■		
Gazania (*Gazania*)	■	■	■		
Larkspur (*Delphinium*)	■		■		■
Marguerite (*Anthemis*)		■	■		
Pink (*Dianthus*)	■	■	■		
Sneezeweed (*Helenium*)	■	■	■		
Stonecrop (*Sedum*)	■		■		
Verbena (*Verbena*)	■				■
Windflower (*Anemone*)	■				
WINTER					
Annuals					
Cineraria (*Senecio*)	■				■
Flowering Cabbage (*Brassica*)	■			■	
Iceland Poppy (*Papaver*)		■	■		
Pansy (*Viola*)	■	■	■		■
Pot Marigold (*Calendula*)		■	■		
Primrose (*Primula*)	■				
Snapdragon (*Antirrhinum*)	■	■	■		
Sweet Pea (*Lathyrus*)	■				■
Violet (*Viola*)	■		■		■
Perennials					
Euryops (*Euryops*)			■		
Hellebore (*Helleborus*)				■	
Primrose (*Primula*)	■	■	■	■	■

BIBLIOGRAPHY

Birren, Faber. *Color & Human Response*. New York: Van Nostrand Reinhold, 1978.

———. *Color Psychology and Color Therapy*. New York: Citadel Press, 1992.

———. *The Symbolism of Color*. New York: Citadel Press, 1988.

Brennan, Georgeanne, and Mimi Luebbermann. *Little Herb Gardens*. San Francisco: Chronicle Books, 1993.

Fairchild, Dennis. *Healing Homes*. Birmingham, Michigan: Wavefield Press, 1996.

Goody, Jack. *The Culture of Flowers*. New York: Cambridge University Press, 1993.

Greenaway, Kate. *The Language of Flowers*. Reprinted from an original manuscript, 1884. England: Dover, 1992.

Hall, Edward T. *The Dance of Life*. New York: Doubleday, 1983.

Hobhouse, Penelope. *Color in Your Garden*. Boston: Little, Brown, 1985.

Jerome, Kate. *Oriental Gardening*. New York: Pantheon Books, 1996.

Kaplan, Rachel, and Stephen Kaplan. *The Experience of Nature*. New York: Cambridge University Press, 1989.

Keville, Kathi, and Mindy Green. *Aromatherapy: A Complete Guide to the Healing Art*. Freedom, California: Crossing Press, 1995.

Kilmer, John. *The Perennial Encyclopedia*. New York: Random House, 1990.

Lancaster, Roy. *What Plant Where*. Boston: Houghton Mifflin, 1995.

Lawson, Andrew. *The Gardener's Book of Color*. Pleasantville, New York: Reader's Digest Association, 1996.

Leff, Herbert L. *Playful Perception*. Burlington, Vermont: Waterfront Books, 1984.

Lehner, Ernst, and Johanna Lehner. *Folklore and Symbolism of Flowers, Plants and Trees*. New York: Tudor Publishing, 1960.

Loewer, Peter. *Tough Plants for Tough Places*. Emmaus, Pennsylvania: Rodale Press, 1992.

Longacre, Bob, and Celeste Longacre. *Sweet Fern*. 6, no. 3, 1996.

Messervy, Julie Moir. *The Inward Garden*. Boston: Little, Brown, 1995.

National Gardening Association. *The National Gardening Association Dictionary of Horticulture*. New York: Penguin Group, 1994.

Pereir, Anita. *The Ward Lock Encyclopedia of Practical Gardening*. London: Ward Lock, 1994.

Phillips, Roger, and Martyn Rix. *Perennials*, Vols. 1 and 2. New York: Random House, 1991.

Sunset Western Garden Book. Menlo Park, California: Lane Publishing, 1988.

Thompson, Angel. *Feng Shui: How to Achieve the Most Harmonious Arrangement of Your Home and Office*. New York: St. Martin's Press, 1996.

Wydra, Nancilee. *Designing Your Happiness, A Contemporary Look at Feng Shui*. Torrance, California: Heian International, 1995.

———. *Feng Shui: The Book of Cures*. Chicago: Contemporary Books, 1996.

INDEX

ABOUT THE AUTHOR

NANCILEE WYDRA

Nancilee Wydra, founder of the Pyramid School of Feng Shui and cofounder of the Feng Shui Institute of America, is the author of *Feng Shui: The Book of Cures* and *Designing Your Happiness: A Contemporary Look at Feng Shui*. She has also written several columns and articles on feng shui, including "Rx's for Living," a nationally syndicated feng shui advice column.

A consultant to developers, businesses, and individuals across the country, Wydra is a lecturer and feng shui educator. She has been a speaker at the national conventions of the American Institute of Architects and the American Booksellers' Association.

The author is interested in receiving photographs of any garden inspired by this book. Send photos or slides to the author at P.O. Box 8001, Vero Beach, FL 32963.

Those interested in receiving more information on feng shui can contact the Feng Shui Institute of America, P.O. Box 488, Wabasso, FL 32970, (561) 589-9900, fax: (561) 589-1611, www.windwater.com, E-mail: Windwater8@aol.com.

BRIDGET SKINNER,
CONSULTING LANDSCAPE DESIGNER

Bridget Skinner has a landscape architecture and garden design firm based in Newport Beach, California. As a practitioner certified by the Feng Shui Institute of America and a graduate of the Western School of Feng Shui, she uses her intellectual and intuitive skills to enhance the experience of place while bringing benefits, harmony, and balance to her clients' interior and exterior environments.

For information on feng shui consultations or exterior design services, please contact Bridget Skinner and Associates, 1048 Irvine Avenue, Suite 495, Newport Beach, CA 92660, (714) 631-3744, bsassoc@ix.netcom.com.